Dear Evan and Karen,

To your family's
financial health!

Sincerely,
Charlie

Endorsements

"Investors today are presented with more opportunities than ever before but also more chances to make serious mistakes. An army of financial professionals claims to offer helpful advice, but their conflicting suggestions often lead to even greater confusion. Charlie Massimo shows us how to cut through the clutter and focus on the key ingredients of investment success."

— Weston Wellington, Vice President of
Dimensional Fund Advisors

"This is an invaluable resource for navigating the convoluted and double-talk world of financial markets. Understanding the emotional aspect of investing, learning to ask the right questions, and managing my investment expectations all become easier when engaging with Massimo's hallmark principles. This book is a MUST READ."

— The Honorable Paul J. Tonna
CEO of Praxis Public Relations
Former Suffolk County Legislator

"I have been a client of Charlie's for over eight years. Throughout our partnership I have been continually comforted by the knowledge that my family's financial future is in the hands of someone who has such a wealth of knowledge of the markets and the discipline to stick to our plan. In a relationship like this, trust is paramount, and Charlie has my complete faith and confidence."

— Michael T. Harris, MD
Senior VP & Chief Medical Officer
Englewood Hospital and Medical Center

"This book should be mandatory reading for anyone that is contemplating hiring an investment advisor. It crystallizes the type of advice you should be getting from the individual who will help invest hard-earned money and describes a process that is vital to attaining financial goals. As a client of CJM, I can attest to the fact that I have slept a lot better for the past ten years than did when I was managing my investments myself."

— GERALD GOLDSTEIN, BUSINESS OWNER

GETTING OFF
THE
STREET

SANE INVESTMENT ADVICE FROM
ONE OF THE NATION'S LEADING
WEALTH MANAGERS

CHARLES MASSIMO

PRESIDENT AND FOUNDER, CJM WEALTH MANAGEMENT

This publication is designed to provide competent and reliable information regarding the subject matter covered. However, it is sold with the understanding that the author and publisher are not engaged in rendering legal, financial, or other professional advice. Laws and practices often vary from state to state and if legal or other expert assistance is required, the services of a professional should be sought.

The author and publisher specifically disclaim any liability that is incurred from the use or application of the contents of this book.

Table of Contents

Introduction:

Getting Off the Street

How many Wall Street horror stories have you heard? Perhaps you saw the recent movie *The Wolf of Wall Street* where investors were deprived of an entire lifetime of their earnings through one company's underhanded dealings with penny stocks. Or you heard about brokers at UBS convincing their clients to take out margin loans to buy securities in Puerto Rico and receiving incentives not only on the securities they sold but also on the loans they contracted as well.[1] How about the investment bankers at Morgan Stanley having "improper influence" over their analysts who rated the stock of Facebook so highly before its initial product offering (IPO)—a stock for which they happened to be the investment banker—only to later be hit with a $5 million fine by the state of Massachusetts after Facebook's share price dropped precipitously, causing investors to lose millions.[2]

You can go to Google right now and enter the terms "financial advisor" and "scandal" and return over six million hits. There are so many shady tactics and burst bubbles, and so many big investment firms cooking the books. Small investors are taking the hit because the focus of too many financial service professionals is on their own greed and profitability. After the Great Recession of 2008 we have all become a little more wary of the spectacular failures of Wall Street. Still, many investors don't know where else to turn, so they are lured back by the warm and fuzzy marketing of large investment houses that convey a false message: "We're part of your family and have your best interest at heart." Sappy, sweet advertising campaigns con investors, who are vulnerable to this style of marketing, and attempt to find new comfort in "family-friendly" portfolio management techniques. What other choice do they have? Some investors leave the market altogether. Others decide to transfer their portfolios to a new financial advisor, someone who will truly have their best interests at heart.

Does such a person exist? Are there advisors out there who will act as your investment fiduciary,[3] meaning they are not only ethically but also legally bound to tell you what is in your best interest? Yes, there are, and I am proud to count myself among that breed of advisor. You always want to work with someone who puts your needs ahead of their own. You want a doctor who is going to prescribe the best medication for your condition, not merely something that is suitable and rewards him in other ways through perks or sponsorship.

It is the same in the financial industry. At my wealth management company, we just brought on a new client who had opened a 529 account to put away money for his child's education. I won't mention the brand name of the fund here but they were charging this individual a fee of two percent a year. The plan that I recommended only charged a fee of .17 percent a year—Figure 7 in Chapter Two shows what an enormous difference fees can make and how quickly they add up to very real money being lost. Both plans were suitable, but which one was in the client's best interest? That is the one that the fiduciary must recommend. I could have offered the fund with the two percent per year in fees and gotten paid a heck of a lot more, but it was not in the client's best interest.

You may be shocked by the details of the journey that led me to work as an investment fiduciary. I know they shocked me. I spent four years at Merrill Lynch before their bail-out and subsequent takeover by Bank of America, and another three years at Smith Barney. In those seven years, it became crystal clear to me that the advisors employed at large brokerage firms are motivated by one thing: to make their company money. These advisors do not act as a fiduciary for their investors. Their recommendations only have to be "suitable" for the investor, not necessarily in their best interest.

When I went into the Merrill Lynch training program in 1996, I was young and naive. I thought that I would be helping clients plan for their future. We were certainly trained well in this two-year program, perhaps the most prestigious of its kind on Wall Street. Unfortunately, the training was all about how to sell. Sell, sell, sell. We were taught how to understand the product we were selling, but not about what makes a client's portfolio successful, balanced, or sustainable. We learned virtually nothing about how to understand the psychology of the client, or how to help them achieve their goals of wealth preservation, life enhancement, and charitable gifting.

It was as simple as this: the more you sold, the faster you got out of the training program and could begin to make "real money." And, what did they want us to sell? Anything that generated a large profit for Merrill Lynch. I remember, in 1997, the company was on a big kick for us to sell a "financial plan." The plan itself was cookie-cutter, and we had to sell fifteen a year to get our full compensation. It came as a nice, bound book but unless you knew how to use it and could take your clients through every page, it was meaningless. One time in training—I was the branch trainer for new hires by then (yes, I had drunk the Kool-Aid)—someone asked, "Why do we have to do this financial plan?" You always had to lead with the plan whether you thought they needed it or not. And, I came back and said, "Well, you shouldn't lead with the plan. You should get to know the client first and find out if the plan is right for them." It just so happens that one of the higher-ups was sitting in on my training session, and boy, did I get into some hot water over that! I was told, "That is not your job! Your job is to sell what we tell you to sell." That was the first time the lightbulb went on in my head—my first *aha* moment, if you will—that we were not fiduciary advisors, we were just brokers. No one was teaching us how to build a relationship with the client or how to watch out for the client's best interests.

In essence, we were forced to sell Merrill Lynch products. For example, if we sold XYZ Mutual Fund and it wasn't a Merrill fund, we would receive a certain number of "credits," whereas if we sold a fund underwritten by Merrill Lynch, we would receive five times that number of credits which would help us get out of training more quickly. Now, don't get me wrong. There are phenomenal brokers and advisors at Merrill Lynch—smart, smart people. But the way we were incentivized, if you really wanted to make money, you were forced to put the firm's interests ahead of your clients, plain and simple. To top it all off, only the very major brokers, who had been at the game a while, made a great living. The rest of us had to sell a lot to survive.

It was the same at Smith Barney, and it is the same everywhere, then as now. Almost every recommendation that is made comes with some conflict behind the scenes. Another example: If we went over certain levels of production we would receive stock options as a kind of bonus. It was an incentive that we didn't have to pay for, and it seemed like a great idea at the time. Until you realized that you were locked in—you couldn't sell these stock options for seven to ten years. And, if you left the company, you would lose them altogether. So if you wanted to retire someday, all you could really afford to care about was increasing Smith Barney's stock price. That was embedded in the raw deal we received.

Now, obviously, any business owner is going to want to increase their own stock price. But how did we get there? At what cost? Every morning we would have what were known as "squawk boxes" during which the analysts would get on the intercom that was chimed into every office and tell you which stock to buy. I remember one morning at Merrill Lynch the announcement came on. I remember it as clear as if it was yesterday: "Tell your clients to back the truck up and buy Boston Chicken stock." This was the kind of boasting comment that made us really believe the analysts knew what they were talking about: "Back the truck up." The only problem was that shortly thereafter, Boston Chicken filed for Chapter 11 bankruptcy in 1998. It was later recapitalized and reemerged as Boston Market, but, in the meantime, investors in that stock got slaughtered. So why should we tell them to back the truck up? Because Merrill Lynch was getting huge fees as investment banker for Boston Chicken.[4] We were, in effect, getting paid off to ignore the indicators of what makes a good investment and simply support the stock at all costs.

How did they get us to ignore such salient facts? We were wined and dined every week in the fanciest of restaurants, with hundred dollar bottles of wine and thousand dollar lunches. If you watch the Academy Award–winning documentary, *Inside Job*, you can see some of the excesses that Wall Street is prone to: indulging in various vices, conspicuous consumption. But, all the cigarette boats and private jets are just a distraction from the fact that advisors are playing the riskiest of games with other people's money.

I, too, was enticed by some of these trappings at one time. In 1998, after building a successful practice at Merrill Lynch, I was lured away by Smith Barney who paid me an upfront six-figure bonus to move. With triplets on the way I jumped at the offer. While I was at Smith Barney I worked with another advisor who was your typical gun-slinger. Here I was, doing my boring asset allocation, earning 10–12 percent a year, while he was trading his Internet and technology stocks earning sometimes 10 percent in a single day! I noticed how much more money he was making with all of those commissions while I was simply making one annual fee. I got sucked in and tried trading the markets, not just for myself but for my clients as well.

For a while it was great . . . easy money during the "dot com" days. Well, we all know what happened then: the bottom fell out. My clients' portfolios tanked and I lost my entire life savings. With newborn triplets, I had to sell my home and move into my in-laws' three-family house. If not for them I don't know what I would have done. It was during that time that I started thinking seriously about leaving the big boys on Wall Street, even though it was during a brutal bear market right after the tragic and disconcerting events of 9/11. The state of the financial industry was in such disarray then (including the departure of seventy percent of the brokers who were in the business at the time). I remember sitting in a meeting when our company spokesperson said, "We know this has been a difficult time, but we need to go back to making money for the firm. So you have to go out and make commissions that will put money in your pockets."

That was exactly what he said. I thought, *Are you kidding me?* I love the financial services industry and I want to stay in this industry. But, no way am I going to do it the way these big Wall Street firms are telling me to do it. I don't want to give advice that only ties back to my own profitability and the profitability of my firm by driving up our stock price. I want to build common-sense portfolios that bring value and grow my business the right way by being a fiduciary and not a broker.

A little more than a year later I convinced my gunslinging colleague that if we really wanted to do the right thing for our clients we needed to start our own firm. We approached our clients and told them about our plans. We even picked a date to resign—it was going to happen on a Friday at 4pm in August. I went first, and called my branch manager to tell him the news. I then waited for my colleague but no word . . . no calls, no emails. He finally called me around 4:30pm to inform me that not only was he staying . . . but if I returned, they would fire me.

Sure enough the next call was from my branch manager who gave me two options. I owed them money from that six-figure bonus they gave me for coming over; as I now knew that wasn't really a bonus but rather a leash. Option One was to repay that money. Option Two was to leave Smith Barney with basically no clients. Now in fairness to my manager at Smith Barney this was money he could have fought me for legally. His just giving me the option to walk away was the greatest gift he could have given me even though I didn't realize it at the time because it allowed me to pursue building a world-class wealth management practice. I worked hard to keep that vision in mind every day, and some days it was hard to keep in mind as I went to my rented office that measured ten feet by ten feet, with no windows and no air, just a phone, a desk and a chair.

It would have been far easier for me to stay at Smith Barney and make a nice career for myself, especially as my two boys had just been diagnosed with autism and the pressure that put on me. There would have been quite an upside to my toeing the line there as opposed to a lot of potential downside to leaving. But, I was driven by my passion to tell my clients things they never heard on Wall Street about how to properly grow and preserve one's wealth. I started to tell my story through seminars every month . . . and the rest, as they say, is history.

That was more than a decade ago, and in the meantime, most investors still have failed to learn that when you work with the big Wall Street firms, it does little to enhance your wealth—quite the opposite. In most cases, it diminishes wealth to a point that many investors may never recover from. It is really only a false security blanket. The truth is that, **when improving the overall financial wealth of their**

clients, most financial advisors spend the majority of their time on the areas that matter least.

There is another approach that you may not have heard about which ensures good returns with acceptable risk and prudent diversification. We call that approach **structured investing**, and you will learn its principles in the following pages. Structured investing is not available through major Wall Street firms for the simple reason that they cannot make money off of it. Since it is not a trading strategy per se, you're not going to see it available in the major wire houses.

What is structured investing?

- Structured investing minimizes excessive portfolio turnover by design, so that investors don't get hit with unwieldy fees—fees that cost investors more than $100 billion per year according to a recent study[5] by Dartmouth economist Kenneth French.

- Structured investing reduces the natural volatility of the market with broadly diversified investments that are put to the test of annual or semiannual rebalancing (more information on diversification and rebalancing will follow in Chapter Three).

- Structured investing maintains a focus on strategy, while consistently seeking new opportunities. Though every client's needs are different, portfolios built on the principles of structured investing share consistent and efficient exposure to the dimensions of higher expected returns.

So why doesn't everybody do it? Because instead of providing an education to individual investors, for the most part, Wall Street and the financial media thrive on pushing investor's emotional hot buttons. Amped-up spokespeople delivering so-called breaking news about a particular company being subject to a major lawsuit, and the continuously running stock ticker at the bottom of financial TV shows are designed to produce a certain hysteria; the feeling that you, as the investor, have to act now. Why? To drive transactions, which result in commissions for your broker, or to sell magazines, which results in making money for advertisers and producers.

It's that simple. We are bombarded with a lot of bad financial ideas on a daily basis, which cumulatively have the effect of convincing us that our investments have to be active in order to reap a decent return. Investors feel that they need to be constantly buying and selling, and that the more risk they take, the more they are going to be rewarded for that risk. In reality, quite the opposite is true. You'll get to know me better in the pages ahead, but I should tell you right now that I am a huge New York Giants fan. So, I use this analogy: If the quarterback, Eli Manning, goes out and plays football without a helmet, he's not going to get paid more for taking that risk because it's a risk that can be minimized. You can do away with that risk because it is unnecessary; it is the same with structured investing. We eliminate those big risks for which you're not being compensated.

It's funny, but I tell people, **you don't need a wealth manager, you need a behavioral investment advisor.** What I mean is that the number one thing that structured investing requires is the ability for an investor to control his or her emotions. That is the most important tool we can have in our investment toolbox. It is natural to worry where your money is. After all, it is a matter of survival. Some clients worry about losing their hard-earned wealth. Others, as we have seen, take unnecessary risks in a misguided effort to beat the market. And, some clients prefer to avoid dealing with their finances altogether. Each of these approaches is motivated by a different emotion. In fact, investing is one of the most emotional things that anyone will do in their life. People have a very difficult time with the emotions around money, which is why a solid wealth management plan is not about the numbers. It is about controlling a client's behavior.

By utilizing the principles of structured investing we can eliminate panic and fear from our financial picture because our investments are based on an enduring philosophy rather than a changeable outlook. In the next chapter, we will see proof that no one among us is a stock picker. Dozens of studies have shown that no one can consistently pick winners and avoid losers. Simply put, we cannot time the market. This is a fact that your broker will not tell you, because it is easier for them to impress you with their past results—which are meaningless in the context of the present and the future—than to connect with you emotionally, and to help you articulate the emotions that we all experience around money. In this book, I will invite you into a deeper exploration of these emotions and the positive possibilities our will-power can provide us with when we counter the prevailing attitudes in the financial services industry.

- **PATIENCE**—the refusal to do the wrong thing at the spur of the moment. Patience is the best way to counter impatience: the desire for the quick buck or 30 percent growth, which is based on flimsy research and unstable conditions.

- **DISCIPLINE**—by following both our own personal discipline and the discipline of a Nobel Prize–winning approach to investing we eliminate the emotional curve that rises through hope and greed only to fall into panic and disappointment.

- **DIVERSIFICATION**—effectively diversifying our portfolios ensures an investment experience that is consistent and one with lower risk and greater returns. This helps us overcome our anxiety: believing that the market can be timed for a single big payday (even if our efforts to do so have failed repeatedly).

- **GOAL-SETTING**—proceeding from the secure base of knowing what we want to achieve in the financial market-place. When we know ourselves financially we no longer need to cover up our failures or experience envy (i.e., wanting what others may appear to have).

At this point in the book you are likely asking yourself, "Can I trust this man?" That is always the crux of the matter in the financial services industry. That is always the unspoken question between client and advisor: Can I trust you? It will rarely, if ever, be spoken by the client, leaving it to the advisor to bring up—and that is why I would like to address this matter.

When you read the pages that follow here, you will see that structured investing is simple enough for a beginner to comprehend, yet complex enough that sophisticated investors will understand why this approach will work for them. All of my clients comment that they don't have a lot of time and that is why they understand the value of delegation. They know they can't do everything, but, if they can find people they trust and can delegate to, they can grow without cloning themselves. I just met with a partner in a big law firm and he told me, "Charlie, I'm not an expert at this. I make a lot of money, but I just keep it in the bank. Because I'm naive about investing—and I know that I am naive. And, I also know that I don't have time to learn about investing. So, I want to find a person I trust and leave it up to them."

Imagine you were to walk into a restaurant and saw that the room was full of people: men and women, of varying nationalities and physical builds, some with glasses and some without (some with hair and some without!), but they were all dressed the same. And, now imagine you were told that these were all financial advisors, and you had to pick which one with whom you want to work. How would you go about it—by speed dating or by choosing a few and hearing them out?

That is the reality facing many people. And, that is why I want you to hear the perspective of someone who got off "the Street" and did an about-face on what he had been trained to do by the large firms; someone who can show you how to have the most successful and meaningful investment experience possible.

Let's get started.

POINTS TO REMEMBER:

► Most financial advisors spend the majority of their time on the areas that matter least when improving the overall financial wealth of their clients.

► Structured investing ensures good returns with acceptable risk and prudent diversification.

► The most important thing an investor can do is learn how to control his or her emotions.

Chapter One:

Patience

A s I mentioned in the introduction, the highest calling of a financial advisor is to be a **behavioral manager**. Of course, your advisor needs to understand how markets work. Advisors need to know about asset allocation and diversification, rebalancing your portfolio, mitigating taxes, etc. But, most of all, they need to know about you. Knowing your individual situation will help them keep your emotions in check so that their wisdom can actually do you some good! It is our emotions that get in the way of long-term financial success, and gaining control over four negative emotions in particular is the most important thing with which your advisor can assist you.

The first of these emotions is *impatience* aka recklessness, reckless abandonment, being compulsive, craving, demanding results, never having enough, never being satisfied. . . . Some people might say what I am describing here is the very essence of investing—why shouldn't I want more, and then more after that? Investors who suffer from impatience are a bit like gamblers: they want to turn a quick profit; they want to double down and get out of the casino after a big win. But we know what happens to those unfortunate people afflicted with a gambling problem. They are back at their favorite table the next week giving it all back and more. **If you think about it, both Las Vegas and Wall Street are built on the losers' money, not the winners' money.** That is how the big brokerage firms continue to exist and thrive, because of all the people who have lost money and because of all the fees that Wall Street collects every year. This is impatience in action.

Two Erroneous Beliefs

Impatience in investing is fueled by two erroneous beliefs, which are related to each other:

1. You believe in your (or your broker's) ability to make security selections that are superior to other people

2. You believe in your (or your broker's) ability to time the markets better than other people

Reread these two statements and be honest with yourself. Where do you fall in this discussion? There is no real middle ground here. Either you believe you (or your broker) can choose securities such as stocks, mutual funds, and bonds better than prevailing wisdom—or you don't. Either you believe you (or your broker) can time the market better than the rest of the professionals in the financial services industry (i.e., you know better when to buy low and sell high—or you don't).

Now, if you do hold one or both of these beliefs, don't worry. You are far from alone! Figure 1 describes the company you may be keeping. Along the vertical axis, you will see the first belief reflected: whether you believe in the ability of an individual to make superior security selections (yes/no). Along the horizontal axis, you will see the second belief reflected: whether you believe in the ability of an individual to effectively time the market (yes/no). Responding to each of these questions yields four possibilities or quadrants:

FIGURE 1

Investor Quadrants[6]

Market Timing

		YES	NO
Security Selection	YES	**NOISE** QUADRANT Most individual investors Financial Journalists	**CONVENTIONAL WISDOM** QUADRANT Most individual investors Financial Journalists
	NO	**TACTICAL ALLOCATION** QUADRANT Pure market timers Asset allocation funds	**INFORMATION** QUADRANT Academics Many institutional investors

Let's look at each of the four quadrants in turn.

The Noise Quadrant

Individuals in the Noise Quadrant believe that they can pick better individual financial instruments than other people (whether they be stocks, bonds, futures, etc.) as well as time the market better than other people. Unfortunately, most of us are in this quadrant—perhaps because we have had success in our chosen professional careers, or because we've always been told we were smart—who knows? But there are a lot of people out there who think they can consistently uncover mispriced investments that will deliver market-beating returns and that they can predict when entire market segments will go up or down.

The fact remains (and our personal experience bears this out) that whatever methods we might use, the vast majority of people in the Noise Quadrant will fail to even match the market, let alone beat it.

So why do some of us remain stuck here? Wall Street is partially to blame because it is in their self-interest to drive multiple transactions, which result in commissions for your broker. The more changes you feel compelled to make to your portfolio, the more active you become, and the richer those individuals get. And, because this strategy seems to be working, the more newsletters, bulletins, email blasts, and hard copy mailings you are likely to receive from them. The hope is that all of these communications will generate the emotion of impatience and you, as the individual investor, will feel forced to respond.

Another chief culprit in generating the "noise" that this quadrant is named for is, as you may have guessed, the media. The media wants to convince you that you can choose better selections than others and time the market better than others because they want to sell you the newspapers and magazines that contain this so-called advice. Instead of providing an education to individual investors, they want to sell advertising that accompanies certain television shows to which viewers will return again and again to receive seemingly crucial and timely pieces of information. This inundation has become especially intense as the media has grown into a twenty-four-hour-a-day, seven-day-a-week phenomenon. To compete, these outlets must push investors' emotional hot buttons in order to maintain their audiences.

Can you imagine the freedom of not having to worry about any of these trumped-up urgencies anymore? That is the feedback that I get from clients when together we have found a way to manage their emotion of impatience. One such client, Marianne, was a widower with a good-sized portfolio of roughly $7 million. Marianne had lost a lot of money with a broker two years prior to our first meeting and had decided she was going to take on the responsibility of managing her portfolio by herself. She subscribed to a dozen or so newsletters and continually watched the financial programs on television (which I won't name here, but you know what they are!). It was at once an all-consuming and a frustrating experience for her. On the one hand, it took up a tremendous amount of her head space. On the other hand, she didn't have the time nor the interest to tend to the markets with this much energy. She later remarked to me that she didn't find it all that "fun," either!

The reality is that investing is a full-time job. If you treat it like a part-time job, those are the kind of results you're going to get. And, why would you want to do that when it's your wealth and your future we're talking about? When we took over Marianne's portfolio, we found the effects of it having been managed by a "part-timer." Because she was just responding to the "breaking news" being pumped out by various media outlets, she had a little bit of her money in this and a little bit in that. She really didn't have a structure behind what she was doing. When I identified that she was living in the Noise Quadrant and revealed our investment philosophy to her, she went from being a skeptical client to one of our most devoted fans.

After we had been working together for roughly three months, Marianne went on a vacation with her grandchildren to Spain. When she returned, she sent me an email that read, "You know, Charlie, that was the first time I have spent ten days away from my portfolio since Albert [her husband] died. It used to be that I was always checking my investments, always checking the markets, but I just didn't do that this time around, which, in my mind, justified my decision to work with you. You have given me a sense of freedom!"

I thanked Marianne for her email and expressed my gratitude that she had come to such an "aha" moment. Then I told her that what we need to do now is keep this going, *to continue being patient.* To fully escape from the Noise Quadrant, we can't confuse entertainment with advice. The financial media is in the entertainment business and their message can compromise anyone's long-term focus. It really is the self-interest of others that prevents most investors from having a successful and consistent investment experience. I told Marianne that, in order to rise above the noise, it was okay to watch her financial investment television shows, but that she should do it with the sound off!

The Conventional Wisdom Quadrant

In the Conventional Wisdom Quadrant, we find subscribers to only one of the two erroneous beliefs depicted on page 15—so a little sanity is being established, but not much! Many members of the financial services industry know from personal experience that they can't time the market swings with any degree of accuracy, but they still believe they can find undervalued securities in whatever sector they choose to apply themselves. In many ways, this reflects the "American dream," the one that says, if you're bright enough and work hard enough, if you have courage and completely dedicate yourself, then you will be successful in a competitive environment. The problem is, with regard to markets that are "efficient" anyway, this isn't really true. Later in the book, we will go into more detail about what I mean by an "efficient market." But, for present purposes, we can simply say: capital markets work. What this means is that while individual people can be wrong about the market, the market as a whole is always right.

Taking this as a starting point, we see that the conventional wisdom approach adds, on average, no value to a portfolio. But, why is this so? Surely there are many situations in which investors and their brokers have scored "big wins"? This is true, but it is only half the picture—the half you hear about, not the half that is swept under the rug by individuals who might want to brag about their successes and omit their failures. Lately, some of these colossal failures have come out in the news. Here is one to consider: Bill Miller was the portfolio manager for a mutual fund that recorded one of the longest "winning streaks" in mutual fund history. Between 1991 and 2005, Miller's fund (measured by total return) beat the S&P 500 index for fifteen consecutive years.[7] Then along came the Great Recession of 2008, and what happened? He gave it all back.

Word on "the Street" is that Bill Miller is back with a new winning streak. Tell that to the many investors in his Value Trust Mutual Fund who thought they were reaping fantastic returns for seventeen years only to wake up to the reality that, if they had simply invested in an S&P index fund, they would have been better off!

You don't have to be running a multibillion-dollar mutual fund to have this kind of experience, of course. You could have an individual brokerage account and pick stocks based on your general understanding of growth industries in our culture. And, you might be right, for a while. You might even pick five great stocks correctly, buying low and selling high . . . until along comes that one stock you get wrong. And, then your loss on that one stock wipes out all of the gains you have made on your five wins.

One of the reasons for this scenario is—you guessed it—impatience! Let's say that among your five stocks in the previous example you had an überwinner, a Google, let's say. How many investors would have the patience to hold onto that stock and make the millions of dollars that we hear about and that make us so envious? The reality is very few individuals would have had the discipline to buy and hold because of the lack of an overall investment philosophy like the kind this book describes, and it doesn't even have to be a stock with a meteoric rise. One of my clients reported buying $1,900 worth of Pier One Imports in 2008 for sixteen cents a share. He ended up with a little under twelve thousand shares. Soon the stock went up to twenty-one cents a share—a profit of roughly $600—more than 33 percent. Not bad! Meanwhile, if my client has stayed the course, just five years later, that stock would have been worth more than $300,000.

It's not that you or your broker can't find undervalued securities. It's that doing so requires an inordinate amount of time and effort. You have to have access to certain information, sophisticated tools and screens, which already have been evaluated on a collective basis. Why reinvent the wheel?

The Tactical Allocation Quadrant

The Tactical Allocation Quadrant finds investors clinging to the opposite error from those in the Conventional Wisdom Quadrant. Here investors and their brokers have let go of their belief that they can

---

FIGURE 2

Asset Class Index Performance 1998–2013[8]

1998	1999	2000	2001	2002	2003	2004	2005	2006	
Large Growth 36.65%	Emerging Markets 66.49%	REITs 26.37%	Small Value 40.59%	5 Year Gov't 12.95%	Small Value 74.48%	REITs 31.58%	Emerging Markets 34.00%	REITs 35.06%	HIGH
S&P 500 Index 28.58%	Small Growth 54.06%	5 Year Gov't 12.60%	REITs 13.93%	REITs 3.82%	Emerging Markets 55.82%	Small Value 27.33%	EAFE 13.54%	Emerging Markets 32.14%	
EAFE 20.00%	Large Growth 30.16%	Inflation (CPI) 3.39%	5 Year Gov't 7.61%	Inflation (CPI) 2.38%	Small Growth 54.72%	Emerging Markets 25.55%	REITs 12.16%	EAFE 26.34%	
Large Value 11.95%	EAFE 26.96%	Small Value -3.08%	Inflation (CPI) 1.55%	Emerging Markets -6.17%	EAFE 38.59%	EAFE 20.25%	Large Value 9.70%	Large Value 21.87%	
5 Year Gov't 10.22%	S&P 500 Index 21.04%	Large Value -6.41%	Emerging Markets -2.62%	Small Value -11.72%	REITs 37.13%	Large Value 17.74%	Small Growth 6.02%	Small Value 21.70%	
Small Growth 4.08%	Large Value 6.99%	S&P 500 Index -9.10%	Large Value -2.71%	EAFE -15.94%	Large Value 36.43%	Small Growth 11.16%	S&P 500 Index 4.91%	S&P 500 Index 15.79%	
Inflation (CPI) 1.61%	Small Value 4.37%	EAFE -14.17%	Small Growth -4.13%	Large Growth -21.93%	S&P 500 Index 28.68%	S&P 500 Index 10.88%	Small Value 4.46%	Small Growth 9.26%	
Small Value -10.04%	Inflation (CPI) 2.68%	Large Growth -14.33%	S&P 500 Index -11.89%	S&P 500 Index -22.10%	Large Growth 17.77%	Large Growth 5.27%	Inflation (CPI) 3.42%	Large Growth 5.97%	
REITs -17.50%	5 Year Gov't -1.76%	Small Growth -24.50%	Large Growth -21.05%	Large Value -30.28%	5 Year Gov't 2.40%	Inflation (CPI) 3.26%	Large Growth 3.39%	5 Year Gov't 3.15%	
Emerging Markets -25.34%	REITs -4.62%	Emerging Markets -30.83%	EAFE -21.44%	Small Growth -34.63%	Inflation (CPI) 1.88%	5 Year Gov't 2.26%	5 Year Gov't 1.35%	Inflation (CPI) 2.54%	LOW

---

find individual undervalued securities, but they retain the belief that they (and only they) can see broad mispricing in entire market sectors.

You see great examples of this kind of mistake every year, if you look at Figure 2 below. This year the "can't lose" sector is real estate . . . until it goes upside down. In recent years, it has been gold. During the Great Recession of 2008, some of my clients asked, "Why aren't you buying me gold?" I remember one client whose son had just graduated with his MBA and had then gone to work at one of the big Wall Street firms. She called me and said, "Charlie, I'm taking my money with you out and I'm putting it all with my son who does gold futures." Now, I wanted to be very careful because we were talking about family here, but, her son had never seen a bear market. Maybe she had other friends

2007	2008	2009	2010	2011	2012	2013	Annualized Returns	
Emerging Markets 39.42%	5 Year Gov't 13.11%	Emerging Markets 78.51%	Small Value 34.59%	5 Year Gov't 9.46%	Large Value 28.03%	Small Growth 47.34%	Small Value 12.09%	HIGH
Large Growth 15.70%	Inflation (CPI) 0.09%	Small Value 70.19%	Small Growth 31.83%	REITs 8.29%	Small Value 20.32%	Large Value 43.19%	Emerging Markets 10.91%	
EAFE 11.17%	S&P 500 Index -37.00%	Large Growth 38.09%	REITs 27.96%	Large Growth 6.42%	Emerging Markets 18.22%	Small Value 40.29%	REITs 10.36%	
5 Year Gov't 10.05%	REITs -37.73%	Small Growth 38.09%	Large Value 20.17%	Inflation (CPI) 2.96%	REITs 18.06%	Large Growth 39.43%	Small Growth 6.27%	
S&P 500 Index 5.49%	Large Growth -39.12%	Large Value 37.51%	Emerging Markets 18.88%	S&P 500 Index 2.11%	EAFE -17.32%	S&P 500 Index 32.39%	5 Year Gov't 5.13%	
Small Growth 4.99%	EAFE -43.38%	EAFE -31.76%	Large Growth 17.64%	Small Growth -4.43%	Large Growth 17.22%	EAFE 22.78%	S&P 500 Index 4.68%	
Inflation (CPI) 4.08%	Small Growth -43.41%	REITs 27.99%	S&P 500 Index 15.06%	Small Value -10.78%	S&P 500 Index 16.00%	REITs 2.47%	EAFE 4.54%	
Large Value -12.24%	Small Value -44.50%	S&P 500 Index 26.46%	EAFE -7.75%	EAFE -12.14%	Small Growth 12.59%	Inflation (CPI) 1.51%	Large Growth 4.22%	
REITs -15.69%	Large Value -53.14%	Inflation (CPI) 2.72%	5 Year Gov't 7.12%	Emerging Markets -18.42%	Inflation (CPI) 1.74%	5 Year Gov't -1.07%	Large Value 2.53%	
Small Value -18.38%	Emerging Markets -55.33%	5 Year Gov't -2.40%	Inflation (CPI) 1.50%	Large Value -19.90%	5 Year Gov't 0.64%	Emerging Markets -2.60%	Inflation (CPI) 2.38%	LOW

who had been holding on to their gold for the past thirty years and were only now starting to make money on it. Whatever the case, gold was being touted as the new cure for present-market doldrums, the new asset class where you can't lose. Well, not only could she lose, but, she lost her shirt in the second quarter of 2013, which happened to be the worst quarter for gold *in ninety-three years.*

The point is that rotating your portfolio through the current "hot" asset class without a discipline or overarching strategy is bound to back-fire. By using the tactical allocation strategy investors are still putting all of their eggs in one basket—they are just swapping out the basket.

The chart on the previous two pages is a lot to look at, huh? Each of these different shades represents a different asset class within the financial markets. What I want to draw your attention to is that not only did no asset class repeat as the highest performing sector for more than two years in a row, but also every asset class shows staggering ups and downs. Find the white boxes, for example, which demonstrate the performance of Emerging Markets. You can see how it goes from the best performing asset class in 2007 to the worst performing asset class in 2008 and back to the best performing asset class in 2009.

The truth is that all asset classes behave like this eventually. These terrifying ups and downs are the result of believing that you can add value by buying when an asset class is undervalued and selling when that asset class is fairly valued again. In reality, however, it is inconsistent to think that individual securities are fairly priced, but the overall market—which is an aggregate of fairly priced individual securities—is not.

The Information Quadrant

This brings us at last to the Information Quadrant. By "information" I mean relying on empirical evidence for which we have decades, or in some cases centuries, of data to back up that information. Having access to this is what transforms you from an investor into an "informed investor"—the highest compliment we can give out around my office!

You may very well have seen a chart like this one delineating the performance of the S&P 500 over the past seventy-five years:

FIGURE 3

Major Market Tops and Bottoms in the S&P 500

Major Tops				Major Bottoms		
DATE	PRICE	GAIN		DATE	PRICE	GAIN
AUG 03, 1956	49.64	N/A		OCT 22, 1957	38.98	-21.5%
DEC 12, 1961	72.64	86.4%		JUN 26, 1962	52.32	-28.0%
FEB 09, 1966	94.06	79.8%		OCT 07, 1966	73.20	-22.2%
NOV 29, 1968	108.37	48.0%		MAY 26, 1970	69.29	-36.1%
JAN 11, 1973	120.24	73.5%		OCT 03, 1974	62.28	-48.2%
NOV 28, 1980	140.52	125.6%		AUG 12, 1982	102.42	-27.1%
AUG 25, 1987	336.77	228.8%		DEC 04, 1987	223.92	-33.5%
JUL 16, 1990	368.95	64.8%		OCT 11, 1990	295.46	-19.9%
MAR 24, 2000	1,527.46	417.0%		OCT 09, 2002	776.76	-49.1%
OCT 09, 2007	1,565.15	101.5%		MAR 09, 2009	676.53	-56.8%

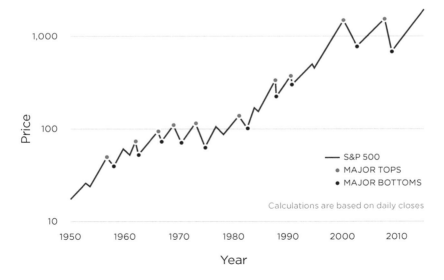

Source: Doug Short/advisorperspectives.com

When informed investors study this chart they see further than some of the most memorable highs and dips of the S&P 500 over the years. They see that what truly counts is not *timing the market*, but *time in the market*. Historical stock market data suggests that *optimism is the realism* when it comes to investing.

We always need to keep it long-term when it comes to financial success. In later chapters, we will be giving plenty of the information from which this quadrant gets its name. For now, I just want you to hear one of the core mantras of this book:

No one can predict the future or accurately guess a good stock.

What does this mean? It means stop searching for the next star money manager and don't speculate on individual stocks with your financial capital. There are no gurus. Instead, let capitalism be your guru. This will later lead us to a key piece of our investment philosophy: owning the entire market in slivers.

To have concerns is natural. Has the market peaked? Has the Dow hit an all-time high? There is always a reason to be fearful as an investor of the market. But we must realize that the permanent trend of the market is always up—the pullback or bear markets are only temporary. There is a great quote by Peter Lynch: "Far more money has been lost by investors preparing for corrections or trying to anticipate corrections than has been lost in the corrections themselves."[9]

The Antidote to Impatience

As we saw in our tour through the four quadrants, consistency is the name of the game when it comes to investing. Consistency and discipline are what it takes to be successful in the market. Together, they constitute *patience*—the antidote to impatience, that emotion we have been trying to control in this chapter.

What is patience and how do we know when we have it? First of all, patience is related to faith; to have one we must have the other. What do we have faith in? In the future, as demonstrated by historical facts like those presented in the S&P chart we just saw. Successful investing is essentially a battle that takes place in the investor's unconscious mind; a battle between faith in the future and fear of the future.

Patience is also known as *not doing the wrong thing on the spur of the moment.* **Changing one's portfolio when one's long-term goals have not changed is virtually always wrong and will depress returns.** To have patience involves the discipline to continue doing the right things for your long-term, goal-focused portfolio. The need for patience is one reason why women make such great investors; speaking in generalities, women (who are controlling more and more of the assets in this country) tend to be less reactive and less risk-prone, while holding more balanced and considered views on life as well as investing. There are additional benefits to having patience as well, including having lower operating expenses. All other factors being equal, lower turnover will result in lower costs (commissions, etc.) that will lead to higher rates of return. The lower turnover motivated by patience also results in lower taxes.

Now, I know what you may be thinking—yes, you agree with the points I have presented above, but is a patient approach . . . well, is it sexy? I would say, it depends what turns you on! If you are looking for sustained, substantive growth plus the added benefit of peace of mind, then I would say: Let your life be exciting and your investments boring!

POINTS TO REMEMBER:

► Over the long run, no one can consistently make better security selections or time the market better than anyone else.

► Investing is a full-time job—if you treat it like a part-time job, you will only get partial results . . . at best.

► For an informed investor what truly counts is not timing the market, but time in the market.

Chapter Two:
Discipline

Discipline may not be the most enticing word. It may not reso-nate with some investors who have only known the market to produce roller-coaster highs and lows. For some clients, however, a disciplined approach to investment management—which is the essence of structured investing—is very appealing. These are the clients who are looking to preserve their wealth in the most prudent manner possible while still reaping all the growth the market has to offer. But, many individuals still hold the popular perception that if their broker isn't constantly trading their portfolio based on the news of the moment, then they as the clients are missing out on the potential for astronomical growth.

This attitude can take hold and persist until worldwide turmoil hits the financial markets. A brutal bear market, such as we saw in 2008, is a time when having a discipline becomes even more crucial. I think 2008 had such an impact on the market, that we really can't talk about it enough. It was one of the worst financial catastrophes in our history, yet not only did some investors live through it, they came out looking phenomenal, proving that the philosophy of structured investing works. How did they do it? We start with what the legendary investor and philanthropist Sir John Templeton said were the four most dangerous words in investing: "This time, it's different."[10]

It's never different. I don't care whether you're talking about the tulip craze of the mid-1600s in Holland, the Wall Street Crash of 1929, or the Great Recession that we just endured. Now, it's true that every bear market teaches us a different lesson. Take the dot.com bubble of the late 1990s, for example. It reinforced the validity of spreading investments across multiple asset classes that move in dissimilar directions. But, the essence of every bear market is the same: individuals running their money up very quickly, thinking their retirement is "all set," without selling any of the stocks or commodities that would create an actual gain. Instead, it merely reflected a paper gain, which very quickly became a paper loss and then some.

As we will see later in this book, one of the aspects of our discipline is periodic rebalancing, which includes the regularly scheduled selling of securities regardless of their current performance, thereby returning a portfolio to a preferred level of risk exposure. This prevents an investor from doing the worst possible thing at the worst possible time: selling at the bottom, and thus dramatically diminishing their ending wealth. A seasoned advisor is someone who can bring this discipline to bear even when it may be unpopular. This is why one of the questions you will want to ask your prospective advisor (covered in Chapter Five) is, "How many bear markets have you been through?"

For example, take the bear market of 1987. Do you remember Black Monday? (This is before that term came to be used for the firing of NFL head coaches the day after the regular season ends.) At a net change of –22.61 percent, it was the single largest loss in the history of the Dow, by a wide margin.[11] I can remember people literally passing out in the office. People thought this was the end of the financial markets as they knew it. As devastating as that day was, however, the lesson I learned is how quickly things can change. And, though people had not forgotten October 19, 1987, by that year's end the market was off on yet another bull run.

The Great Recession of 2008 was an extreme example, but the fact is that many market movements are sharp and unsettling. We think a particular bear market is worse because we're older and that much closer to retirement. We may fear it more, but, again that brings us back to emotions that have to be controlled, rather than actions that have to be taken. When investors experience upheaval, their advisors shift into crisis-management mode while they strive to reassure clients about their investments and financial futures. However, for most of my clients, so-called "scares" are a nonevent. They know if they call me that I'm going to tell them that this has very little to do with their long-term objectives. Those who have been with me for a while do not even panic at all.

I'll bet discipline is looking better and better about now! Do you remember in the previous chapter when I said, "Changing one's port-folio when one's long-term goals have not changed is virtually always wrong and will depress returns"? At the time, I was advocating the virtue of patience, to which the virtue of discipline is closely related. If patience is the decision to not do something wrong in the short term, discipline is the decision to continue doing the right things for your long-term, goal-focused portfolio. By sticking to your discipline, you avoid the negative emotion of *regret*.

Where Does Regret Come From?

In Chapter One, we talked about the Noise Quadrant. The inves-tor who resides within this quadrant tracks the movements of Wall Street closely through their favorite media outlets, reacting to what is portrayed as "news" though really it is entertainment designed to sell advertising and increase viewership. This noise preys on our emotions;

powerful forces that can cause us to do the exact opposite of what we should. Our emotions lead us to buy high and sell low!

Consider the following graph, called the emotional curve of investing. You know how your stomach feels on a roller coaster? That gut-wrenching sense of fear and uncertainty is the same experience felt by many investors. We start off to the left when we get a hot tip regarding a particular investment. We may not buy the security right away—perhaps because we can still feel the queasiness from our last roller-coaster ride. Nonetheless, we track the subject of our interest, a stock for example, as its price rises. When our confidence becomes strong enough, we buy . . . but, then what happens?

FIGURE 4

The Emotional Curve of Investing

GREED / BUY

HOPE / IDEA

FEAR

DISAPPOINTMENT

PANIC / SELL

Source: CEG Worldwide

Almost immediately, the stock starts to go down. When it does, fear begins to creep into our mind that we have made the wrong decision. If it continues to go down, we bargain with the market, saying,

"If only this stock will return to the level at which I bought it, I will sell it and no one will have to be the wiser. I'm okay with breaking even and I have learned my lesson!"

Instead, the stock continues to plunge, and because we have been cut off from any sense of discipline, we have no way of making the correct decision when to sell. Instead of relying on a strategy, we sell at the point when we can no longer take it emotionally—which happens to coincide with the stock being at its all-time low. Then, of course, not long after we have divested ourselves of this stock, new information comes out and the stock races to an all-time high. What went wrong?

We are all poorly wired for investing. When we get emotionally involved in what is going on in the markets, we are reduced to little more than guessing, or gambling. If we can control our emotions however, through the down markets and the up markets, our chances of achieving the long-term results we desire improve significantly. **This is because investing is simple . . . it's just not easy.** The opposite of the emotional curve of investing is the discipline of structured investing, which this book details.

Without a Discipline You Have to Be Right Twice

In our previous example, we followed the emotional curve of investing through the process of buying (and losing on) one stock. But what about when the entire market goes through that roller coaster–like undulation, as in the bear markets I described earlier? This is when having a discipline becomes even more crucial. In a bull market, all too often investors think they are smarter than the market. It is at those times that people take more risks than they should; they go away from their discipline. When we invest with discipline, on the other hand, and invest prudently, we can always make money regardless of the situation—even in a bear market.

But, here's the thing: **to get the full returns of the market on a consistent basis, you have to be fully invested the entire time**. In order to get the ten-year return of a particular investment, you have to be invested for the full ten years. You can't pick and choose when you should go into this or that particular fund or stock. You have to take the volatility of that portfolio to get the full return. This is the essence of the disciplined approach that always works, provided you are properly diversified. I will never promise my client that I will provide them with the best return in any given year. But, anyone who follows our type of discipline has a likelihood of receiving far greater lifetime returns than the vast majority of their peers, and I will say that with very strong confidence.

On the next page is a graph that shows what happens when we stray from our discipline. Let's say, for example, that you invested $1,000 in an S&P 500 index fund from 1970 till today. If you remained fully invested in that security over the entire period, you would enjoy a yearly return of almost 10 percent (and when that figure is compounded, as we will see in the section on volatility, your returns would actually far exceed 10 percent). If, however, you were to withdraw your investment from this security for even one day, and that day was the security's best performing day over the time span being discussed, your yearly return would go down nearly half a percentage point. If you missed the best fifteen days, and keep in mind, this is over a thirty-two-year period—so over 10,000 days, if you missed only fifteen of them and those were the best performing days, your return would go down 2.5 percent. If you missed the twenty-five best performing days of this security, you might have been just as well served by investing your money in U.S. T-bills, which are often thought of as the least risky and least glamorous of all potential investments.

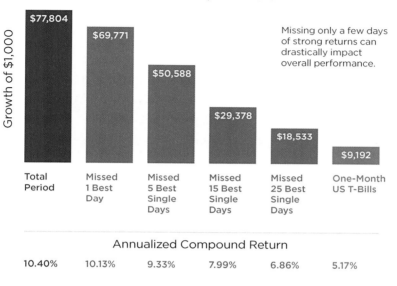

FIGURE 5

Reacting Can Hurt Performance[12]
Performance of the S&P 500 Index, 1970–2013

Growth of $1,000

- Total Period: $77,804
- Missed 1 Best Day: $69,771
- Missed 5 Best Single Days: $50,588
- Missed 15 Best Single Days: $29,378
- Missed 25 Best Single Days: $18,533
- One-Month US T-Bills: $9,192

Missing only a few days of strong returns can drastically impact overall performance.

Annualized Compound Return

Total Period	Missed 1 Best Day	Missed 5 Best Single Days	Missed 15 Best Single Days	Missed 25 Best Single Days	One-Month US T-Bills
10.40%	10.13%	9.33%	7.99%	6.86%	5.17%

The opposite of remaining fully invested is called *chasing returns.* In up markets, this is born of the impatience we discussed in the previous chapter—the desire for fast and easy money, quickly turned around. In down markets, chasing returns is motivated by fear and uncertainty. In both cases, it leads to the emotion of regret and needs to be countered with the virtue of discipline.

Now, the nervousness that bear markets engender is certainly understandable. I get it! It can be draining, and that is when you need to know that your advisor is going through the experience with you. During the Great Recession of 2008, it wasn't just the impact of that bear market on my own personal life and that of my family that kept me up at night. It was the fact that my clients' very livelihoods were at stake. Even I asked myself, "What if Templeton was wrong? What if it *is* different this time?" It is at times like those that discipline needs to be adhered to more than ever. It is at those times that I had to call *my* mentors; I had to go back and read history and see that these things had happened before. That year-and-a-half was a brutal time, but, I think we all came out of it stronger emotionally, and our bonds as client and advisor were stronger.

I only had one client during that period tell me, "Charlie, I'm getting out. I can't take it anymore." At first, I echoed his concerns and shared my own challenges of staying focused on the bigger picture, reminding him of the goals that we were trying to achieve ten, twenty, thirty years down the road. I tried to show him what a self-defeating action it would be to exit the market at its bottom. Successful investing is essentially a battle that takes place in an investor's unconscious mind, a battle between faith in the future and fear of the future. Like I said in the previous chapter, historical stock market data suggests that optimism is the realism when it comes to investing. Finally, I told him, "If you get out now, I will be of no use to you when you call me up and say, 'Charlie, when should I get back in?' Because, now you have to be right twice, when to get out and when to get back in, and I don't know anyone who's that smart."

What is Our Discipline?

Investors' memories tend to be short! Every bubble reminds us of the importance of discipline, and then that memory fades, but discipline always comes into play. What is this discipline that economists such as the Nobel Prize-winning academic Eugene Fama espouse? It includes many elements which we have and will continue to touch on, such as:

- **DIVERSIFICATION:** Since we can never know which sectors are about to "outperform" others, and which will fade away, diversification is a way to spread the risk and reward both within and across asset classes. Broad diversification eventually captures the full ride of all the sectors, but with somewhat muted volatility at any given moment.

- **ASSET CLASS ALLOCATION:** Otherwise known as "owning the market in slivers," asset allocation involves purchasing every security in an asset class so as to get the true advantage of "buying and holding," as opposed to being at the mercy of the volatility of individual securities.

- **REBALANCING:** Although it may seem counter-intuitive, rebalancing means you sell assets that have risen in value and buy more assets that have dropped in value. The purpose of rebalancing is to move a portfolio back to its original target allocation. This relieves volatility and restores strategic structure in the portfolio, thereby putting you back on track to pursue your long-term goals.

One word that you will notice in each of these three strategies is *volatility*. Rebalancing, diversification, and asset class allocation all have the effect of countering volatility. Volatility is really what we are talking about when we are talking about regret. And, here's the good news: **Less volatility equals greater wealth**. It is a simple and straightforward formula! It's like what I always say around the office: stock picking is a game of regret. That's the essence of the emotional curve of investing right there. You always are either selling too soon or too late, and you're always regretting what you did.

Volatility is also present in the graph in Figure 5, which shows the adverse results of having missed the best days in an individual security's performance. In that figure, it mentions that all results are measured by what is called an **annualized compounded return**. What this means is that if you have two investment portfolios with the same average returns, the portfolio with less volatility that results from utilizing effective rebalancing, diversification, and asset class allocation will have a greater compounded rate of return.

Let's look at an example to bring this to life. Two portfolios worth $100,000 begin Year 1. Portfolio #1 goes up 10 percent every year for three years. Portfolio #2 goes up 20 percent in the first year, then down by 10 percent, then up again by 20 percent. Both portfolios should show an equal net gain of 30 percent after the three-year period, correct?

FIGURE 6

Portfolio Return Comparison

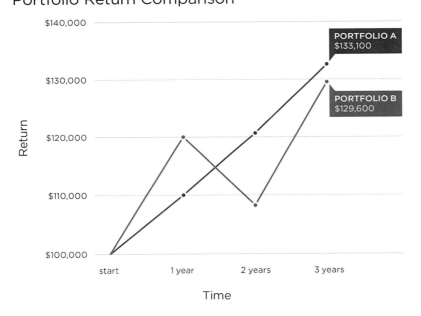

The graph in Figure 6 shows that not all gains are created equal. When comparing two portfolios with the same historical average annual return, the one with the lower volatility in market value will have the higher cumulative rate of return, preserving more of the portfolio's value. Managing volatility is particularly crucial during a market downturn, because, after experiencing a loss, a portfolio must earn an even higher return in future periods to fully recover to its previous level.

Over time, if a portfolio is designed to have as little volatility as necessary to achieve your goals, it will provide a smoother, less emotional ride. Remember the roller coaster we were on earlier in this chapter? In fact, we have a choice how extreme to make those highs and lows. Unless you are an inveterate thrill-seeker, you will see that not only does the route taken by Portfolio #1 aid your ability to sleep at night, but it also gets you where you want to go much more securely. Applying discipline is the answer not only to successful investing, but also to a carefree turn of mind as well. What a sigh of relief!

And, Oh, Those Fees!

If the roller-coaster ride of active investing is one reason to turn to structured investing, the fees of overactive investing is another. You may be thinking, "Fees? Fees are a part of life . . . they're just the cost of doing business." Well, as I mentioned in the Introduction, investors spend over $100 billion annually trying to beat the market.

That's right, *100 billion dollars.* In a study I referenced previously, the Dartmouth economist Kenneth French estimated that those were the costs of active management[13] based on fees you may be aware of and those you may not be aware of. For example, you may understand that your mutual fund has a load fee (to put more money into the product) or a redemption fee (to take money out). But, did you know that you are also paying "distribution fees," "management fees," and "shareholder service fees" which can cover custodial, legal, accounting, and administrative expenses?

You can request a two-hundred-page document from your mutual fund company called the Statement of Additional Information (SAI) which delineates all of the fees that are deducted from your fund assets. However, if you're like most people, you won't have the time or patience to read it. Nonetheless, these fees are reflected in your reduced account balances. Take a look at the following graph which shows how dramatic a difference even 1 percent in annual fees can make over time:

FIGURE 7

Assumed 6.5% Annualized Return
Over 30 Years

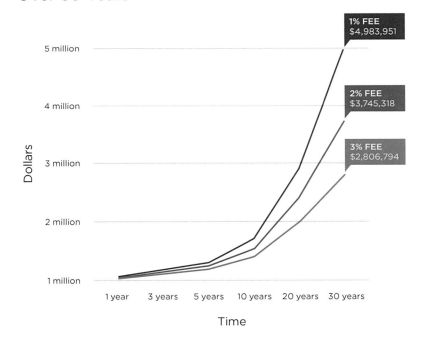

Over long time periods, high management fees and expenses can be a significant drag on wealth creation, not only in terms of incurring higher operating expenses, but also in terms of the higher taxes that such overactive investing invites. And, besides that, it doesn't even work! That's $100 billion spent trying to beat the market . . . and failing!

For example, in a study performed in 2008[14]—the most comprehensive of its kind—advanced analysis was used to measure the performance of active mutual funds over a thirty-two-year period, from 1975–2006. Researchers found that, after expenses (i.e., fees), less than 1 percent of actively managed funds did better than merely investing in the S&P 500 index!

FIGURE 8

Mutual Funds Performance 1975–2006[15]

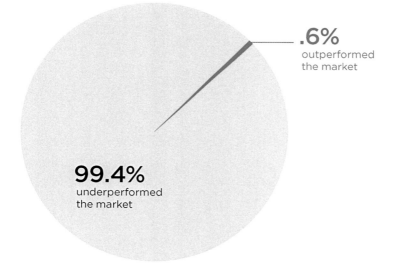

.6%
outperformed
the market

99.4%
underperformed
the market

Let me make one final point before this chapter comes to a close. Structured investing is practicing strict discipline that doesn't change, regardless of market conditions. Structured investing minimizes volatility without minimizing returns. However, structured investing doesn't mean that you and your advisor don't have effective, ongoing communication. You should always expect outstanding service from any financial advisor you choose. Your phone calls should be returned that day, you should receive quick and complete responses to all your questions, and you should be able to meet with your advisor as often as you wish. Structured investing shouldn't prevent your advisor from checking in with you many times a year. It simply means that when they do, they are talking to you about the things that are most important in your life and making sure to keep track of the long-term goal versus talking about the latest gimmick to create a short-term return that will soon disappear.

POINTS TO REMEMBER:

► The four most dangerous words in investing are: "This time, it's different."

► Changing one's portfolio when one's long-term goals have not changed is virtually always wrong.

► Over long periods of time, high management fees and expenses (and the higher taxes they incur) can be a significant drag on wealth creation.

Chapter Three:

Diversification

Alll of the so-called negative emotions that we have been trying to control—so that positive outcomes might emerge—are really just varieties of the biggest negative emotion there is: *fear*. In the case of the financial markets, what are we afraid of? We are afraid that we cannot control the future. The desire to predict how our money will grow and the fear that we cannot control this gives rise not only to impatience and regret, which we covered in the previous two chapters, but also to *anxiety*, which this chapter will address.

You hear this kind of thinking all the time: people don't want to put their money into the market because they got burned before. This happened a lot in 2008. People wanted to throw in the towel, and who could blame them? When a bear market occurs, it is human nature to want to keep your money safe. However, there is a big difference between keeping your money safe and losing money. For example, people say, "I would rather earn zero percent interest in a money market account than lose principal." Putting your hard-earned cash into a money market account is really no better than stuffing it into a mattress or hiding it in a coffee can. You feel like you aren't losing any money, but, in reality, you are losing money every year because of inflation. You just don't see the loss registered in the same way as you might see it on a brokerage statement.

Every year that your money is doing nothing for you it might as well be evaporating. People think that when they retire their costs will go down, but, actually, the daily costs of living go up significantly; not only the cost of health care, but going out and buying food because now you're home every day, or all those additional trips to the gas pump because you have so much more leisure time. And, it is precisely those items of discretionary spending that go up the most in cost.

For example, in 1990, the average cost of a gallon of gas was $1.34 per gallon.[16] What is it now, three times that? So, for every dollar you put in a money market account in 1990, you now need three dollars to get the same amount of gas to travel and do the things you want to do. Where are those other two dollars going to come from? You didn't earn them while the money was just sitting in a money market account. This is why when people take those negative feelings over the futility of the stock market, the feeling that they want to give up and pull out all of their investments, they are really giving into anxiety more than prudent thinking. Because, when you keep your money in a money market account you're just exchanging one risk for another and that's the risk of running out of money.

My father-in-law, God bless him, brought his entire family over from Greece. That's probably the biggest risk anybody can ever take in their life. But, when he got to America and established himself, he would never invest in the stock market. He kept all of his money in CDs (certificates of deposit, which typically earn in the neighborhood of 3 percent interest per year.) Any time the market would go down, he would say to me, "See, I didn't lose a dime!" To which I had to say as respectfully as I could, "But, Dad, look how much money you would have made if you had put that same money in the stock market when you came over in 1970. You would have ten times the money versus keeping the money in a CD!"

My father-in-law took a gigantic risk with his life, which paid off tremendously, but he experiences a great deal of superstition when it comes down to investing. He is far from alone among people who take no risks with their money. You hear people say this all the time, "Every time I put my money in the market, the market goes down." It's the same as when people say, "I don't want to go to the Giants game with you, Charlie, because every time I go, they lose!" This all amounts to what psychologists call magical thinking. It's akin to a five-year-old traveling in the back of a car late at night who thinks the moon is following them.

So, what is following you: the memory of that last, hot stock tip that faded like a shooting star? Or, the time when you put all of your money into one area of the market, be it tech stocks or gold, and then, as the financial world inevitably turned, you found yourself on the wrong end of a banner year in a different sector?

What we always have to remember is that we are not seeking the lone meteoric stock to invest in, because you know what happens to meteors, right? They fall to earth just as fast as they rise. This is what marks structured investing as a process so very different than a simple "buy and hold" strategy.

I recently had a similar conversation with a friend. He said, **"I bought and held Lehman Brothers and Bear Stearns through 2008** and look what it got me—those companies are no longer in business!" This is when I always have to clarify that, that's right, buying and holding individual stocks doesn't work. But, when you buy and hold asset classes, they always come back. Did my investors own Citibank, Bear Stearns, and Lehman Brothers in 2008? Yes, but they were a fraction of our holdings, not 20 percent of our portfolio like this gentleman's. He's right. That would be almost impossible to recover from.

Investing in individual stocks places us in the Noise Quadrant that we examined back in Chapter One where I debunked the myth that we, as individual investors, can somehow pick stocks better than others who have superior tools and training, and who still don't exceed the basic averages of the market. We also don't want to chase the hot asset class, which is the cardinal sin of those in the Tactical Allocation Quadrant, because again, as we saw in Figure 2, what is up one year—say, International Large Cap stocks, or US real estate—will just as surely be down the next. What we want to counter the ups and downs of the various asset classes of the market, and the volatility of individual stocks within a single asset class is **diversification**. Diversification is the antidote to anxiety.

What is Diversification?

Diversification is a buzz word in the investment industry. It receives a lot of press due to the maximum benefits an investor can potentially gain from it. Even though the concept is enjoying newfound popularity, diversification is a time-tested and proven performance strategy. In essence, diversification means spreading the risk and reward within and among asset classes. As we saw in Chapter One, we can never know which asset classes are about to "outperform" others or which will fade away. Broad diversification eventually captures the full ride of all the asset classes, along with somewhat muted volatility at any given moment.

You will remember that old bugaboo, volatility, from our previous discussion. Volatility = bad. Capturing broad market forces, while reducing the excess uncompensated risk arising in individual stocks = good! Diversification reduces the risk in which we place our portfolio so that, even though we can't control the markets, we can control our finances in a way that we never have before. This is how diversification creates an investment portfolio that allows investors to financially meet their goals and objectives while sleeping well at night. No more hopelessness, and no more anxiety!

If diversification can really do all of these things, why wouldn't we diversify? Well, for one thing, we may feel an allegiance to a particular stock or set of stocks. Maybe it has "delivered" for us before and now we can't release our feeling of attachment for it. This, as you can imagine, is another emotion that has to be managed, and when we turn to the concept of rebalancing later in this book we will see how such sentimental attachments can be worked with.

Another reason people may not diversify is because many investors have a large part of their investment capital in their employer's stocks. Rationally, they may understand they are taking too much risk, but they still don't do anything about it. Instead, they justify holding these positions because they fear they would have to pay large capital gains taxes if they sold, or they imagine the stocks are just about to take off, or they would feel "disloyal" if they sold.

These are two reasons why people don't diversify. Then there is another category of investors: those who think they have diversified but, in fact, have done so ineffectively. *Ineffective diversification* occurs when one has many different investments but they tend to move together. For example, most investors think diversification means owning IBM, GE, Coke, and Pfizer, etc. However, when one of these stocks moves up or down, the others will move in tandem because they all take on the same characteristics. Or, to put it another way, they are all in the same asset class; in this case, the asset class known as domestic large cap stocks. Let's use the example of my friend who was complaining about buy and hold earlier in this chapter. If he had only invested in Bear Stearns, Citibank, and Lehman Brothers, then yes, his portfolio was going to underperform. But, if his financial sector stocks were part of a vast portfolio that included the best performing asset classes of 2008 as well, then his losses would not nearly have been so resounding.

The major risk to an ineffectively diversified portfolio is that, because these investments share similar risk factors, all the assets may move down at the same time, creating a potentially large loss that many investors will not be able to recover from. Harry Markowitz, the 1990 Nobel Prize-winner in economics for contributions to Modern Portfolio Theory, taught us that investing in various stocks with similar characteristics is the same as if you didn't diversify at all. If you were to leave your portfolio built around these stocks, all from the same asset group, you would be privy to the same emotional roller-coaster ride that we rode in the last chapter. Ineffective diversification puts an investor at severe risk for not accumulating enough assets to help with a comfortable retirement. While all diversification is good, certain types are much better.

Effective Diversification

In the previous section, I mentioned Modern Portfolio Theory, which was developed at the University of Chicago by Harry Markowitz and Merton Miller and later expanded by Stanford professor William Sharpe. All three later went on to win the Nobel Prize for their contribution to investment methodology. Modern Portfolio Theory states that for every level of risk, there is one optimal combination of investments that will give you the highest rate of return.[17] This is how we decide which investments to own and in what combination. The range of portfolios exhibiting this optimal risk/reward trade-off forms what is known as the **efficient frontier**. The efficient frontier is determined by calculating the expected rate of return, standard deviation, and correlation coefficient for each asset class and using this information to identify the portfolio with the highest expected rate of return at each incremental level of risk.

The mathematical calculations necessary to determine the range of efficient portfolios can be overwhelming. You can find a number of software programs that will help do the calculations and working through each of them will help you understand the end result. (You can also call my office if you would like the formulas to calculate each step on your own.) However, if you are working with an advisor who understands Modern Portfolio Theory, you do not need to know how to calculate each of these steps. It's like buying that Citizen Eco-Drive watch that Eli Manning is the spokesperson for (okay, last Giants reference, I promise!). You don't have to know how the watch works in order to derive the benefits from the way it looks and the information it gives you—and the way people look at you when you're wearing it!

The bottom line is that developing a strategic portfolio is mathematical in nature. It may appear daunting, but it is really just an expression of logic. In other words, it is common sense even if it appears counterintuitive to conventional and over-commercialized investment thinking. Unfortunately, the concepts of Modern Portfolio Theory and the efficient frontier are either misused or ignored by the majority of investment advisors and individual investors. Instead, they base their decisions on a firm's research (which may be the same firm that is underwriting or providing the investment banking for the same security—buyer beware!), or on what they read or hear in the media.

As we saw in Chapter One, market timing and stock selection have very little, if anything, to do with the success of an investment portfolio. Yet, the majority of investment advisors and the investment public spend their time trying to time the market and successfully pick individual stocks. What Markowitz et al. have taught us is that to diversify effectively we have to combine asset classes that don't move in tandem with one another. This will help us benefit from what is known as *dissimilar price movements*. Dissimilar price movement diversification protects you from having all your investments go down at the same time.

Let's revisit a chart from Chapter One:

FIGURE 2

Asset Class Index Performance 1998–2013[8]

	1998	1999	2000	2001	2002	2003	2004	2005	2006
HIGH	Large Growth 36.65%	Emerging Markets 66.49%	REITs 26.37%	Small Value 40.59%	5 Year Gov't 12.95%	Small Value 74.48%	REITs 31.58%	Emerging Markets 34.00%	REITs 35.06%
	S&P 500 Index 28.58%	Small Growth 54.06%	5 Year Gov't 12.60%	REITs 13.93%	REITs 3.82%	Emerging Markets 55.82%	Small Value 27.33%	EAFE 13.54%	Emerging Markets 32.14%
	EAFE 20.00%	Large Growth 30.16%	Inflation (CPI) 3.39%	5 Year Gov't 7.61%	Inflation (CPI) 2.38%	Small Growth 54.72%	Emerging Markets 25.55%	REITs 12.16%	EAFE 26.34%
	Large Value 11.95%	EAFE 26.96%	Small Value -3.08%	Inflation (CPI) 1.55%	Emerging Markets -6.17%	EAFE 38.59%	EAFE 20.25%	Large Value 9.70%	Large Value 21.87%
	5 Year Gov't 10.22%	S&P 500 Index 21.04%	Large Value -6.41%	Emerging Markets -2.62%	Small Value -11.72%	REITs 37.13%	Large Value 17.74%	Small Growth 6.02%	Small Value 21.70%
	Small Growth 4.08%	Large Value 6.99%	S&P 500 Index -9.10%	Large Value -2.71%	EAFE -15.94%	Large Value 36.43%	Small Growth 11.16%	S&P 500 Index 4.91%	S&P 500 Index 15.79%
	Inflation (CPI) 1.61%	Small Value 4.37%	EAFE -14.17%	Small Growth -4.13%	Large Growth -21.93%	S&P 500 Index 28.68%	S&P 500 Index 10.88%	Small Value 4.46%	Small Growth 9.26%
	Small Value -10.04%	Inflation (CPI) 2.68%	Large Growth -14.33%	S&P 500 Index -11.89%	S&P 500 Index -22.10%	Large Growth 17.77%	Large Growth 5.27%	Inflation (CPI) 3.42%	Large Growth 5.97%
	REITs -17.50%	5 Year Gov't -1.76%	Small Growth -24.50%	Large Growth -21.05%	Large Value -30.28%	5 Year Gov't 2.40%	Inflation (CPI) 3.26%	Large Growth 3.39%	5 Year Gov't 3.15%
LOW	Emerging Markets -25.34%	REITs -4.62%	Emerging Markets -30.83%	EAFE -21.44%	Small Growth -34.63%	Inflation (CPI) 1.88%	5 Year Gov't 2.26%	5 Year Gov't 1.35%	Inflation (CPI) 2.54%

When I introduced this chart I wrote that if your eyes follow the white boxes for Emerging Markets you can see how investing in only one asset class creates volatility. You can do this for any of the asset classes that you like. Consider the black boxes that show the performance of the S&P 500, for example. We may be used to thinking that Emerging Markets are inherently risky, but the S&P 500, now that's a safe bet! Not true according to this chart; every individual asset class exposes an investor to volatility if all of your eggs are in one basket. If, on the other hand, you look at any particular year, you will see that (with the exception of 2008) if you were evenly invested

2007	2008	2009	2010	2011	2012	2013	Annualized Returns	
Emerging Markets 39.42%	5 Year Gov't 13.11%	Emerging Markets 78.51%	Small Value 34.59%	5 Year Gov't 9.46%	Large Value 28.03%	Small Growth 47.34%	Small Value 12.09%	HIGH
Large Growth 15.70%	Inflation (CPI) 0.09%	Small Value 70.19%	Small Growth 31.83%	REITs 8.29%	Small Value 20.32%	Large Value 43.19%	Emerging Markets 10.91%	
EAFE 11.17%	S&P 500 Index -37.00%	Large Growth 38.09%	REITs 27.96%	Large Growth 6.42%	Emerging Markets 18.22%	Small Value 40.29%	REITs 10.36%	
5 Year Gov't 10.05%	REITs -37.73%	Small Growth 38.09%	Large Value 20.17%	Inflation (CPI) 2.96%	REITs 18.06%	Large Growth 39.43%	Small Growth 6.27%	
S&P 500 Index 5.49%	Large Growth -39.12%	Large Value 37.51%	Emerging Markets 18.88%	S&P 500 Index 2.11%	EAFE -17.32%	S&P 500 Index 32.39%	5 Year Gov't 5.13%	
Small Growth 4.99%	EAFE -43.38%	EAFE -31.76%	Large Growth 17.64%	Small Growth -4.43%	Large Growth 17.22%	EAFE 22.78%	S&P 500 Index 4.68%	
Inflation (CPI) 4.08%	Small Growth -43.41%	REITs 27.99%	S&P 500 Index 15.06%	Small Value -10.78%	S&P 500 Index 16.00%	REITs 2.47%	EAFE 4.54%	
Large Value -12.24%	Small Value -44.50%	S&P 500 Index 26.46%	EAFE -7.75%	EAFE -12.14%	Small Growth 12.59%	Inflation (CPI) 1.51%	Large Growth 4.22%	
REITs -15.69%	Large Value -53.14%	Inflation (CPI) 2.72%	5 Year Gov't 7.12%	Emerging Markets -18.42%	Inflation (CPI) 1.74%	5 Year Gov't -1.07%	Large Value 2.53%	
Small Value -18.38%	Emerging Markets -55.33%	5 Year Gov't -2.40%	Inflation (CPI) 1.50%	Large Value -19.90%	5 Year Gov't 0.64%	Emerging Markets -2.60%	Inflation (CPI) 2.38%	LOW

across the range of diversified options, your gains would have always well-outpaced any losses. Since it is impossible to know which asset classes will perform best in the coming years, diversified investors are those who take a balanced approach and stick with it despite the volatility inherent in the markets. This is yet another variant of "not timing the market" and it is called **asset class investing**, one of the linchpins of structured investing.

With structured investing, we don't chase the hot asset class. If you combine asset classes that move in opposing directions, such as large cap stocks and small cap stocks, then the total risk to the portfolio is lowered and returns will be enhanced. Most people believe that diversification reduces returns, when really the opposite is true: effective diversification enhances returns:

FIGURE 9

Effective vs. Ineffective Diversification

INEFFECTIVE

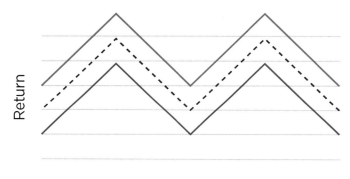

Time

EFFECTIVE

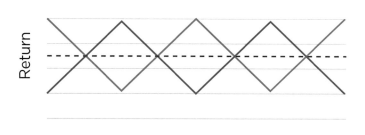

Time

—— ASSET A
----- ASSETS A & B
—— ASSET B

The charts above exemplify how combining two different assets that exhibit similar patterns of performance (ineffective diversification) will always lead to lower returns than when two different assets that exhibit different patterns of performance are combined (effective diversification). In addition, the "ride" is so much smoother!

Even those investors who understand and seek effective diversification often use the wrong tools, such as traditional retail funds to try and create an effectively diversified portfolio, while the correct and most effective tools to use are known as **asset class funds**. Asset class funds, once limited to wealthy investors and large investment funds, are now available to just about every investor; you just need to know where to look for them. There are a limited number of financial advisors throughout the country that specialize in passively managed, asset class funds. One place you might want to start your search is Dimensional Fund Advisors (dfaus.com). The effort you put into finding this type of advisor will go a long way toward securing your financial future.

When you do find the advisor with whom you feel comfortable working, they should have a discipline and a process to take you through. Chapter Five covers this in more detail, but diversification is one of the key tools that they should be using to ensure the productivity and longevity of your portfolio. You can see in the illustration that follows the typical portfolio I see when I first begin working with a client: US stocks and bonds, that's it. Through a four-step process, we begin to gradually shift the emphasis of this typical portfolio to first include US treasuries, then a wider variety of stocks including US Small Cap and US Value Stocks (as specifically recommended by the "Three Factor Model"[18] developed by Eugene Fama and Kenneth

French), and eventually to a well-diversified portfolio built to sustain gains and weather any losses that may be received.

Global Diversification

You can see in Figure 10 that this transformation of the typical portfolio includes nearly 25 percent international securities. I don't know what your reaction is to that, but if you're like many of my clients you may instinctively resist investing overseas to this degree. Investors in the US do tend to favor stocks and bonds of US companies. Maybe it's because we live here? Many find it much more comfortable emotionally to invest in firms that they know and whose products they use rather than in companies located on another continent. Yet, the US financial market represents less than half of the total investable capital market worldwide. In fact, the international equity market has grown from 34 percent to 53 percent of what is known as *global market capitalization* between the years 1970 and 2006—and by the year 2050 international investments are projected to occupy 83 percent of the world's total securities.[19]

The fact is, overseas investments can help you grow your wealth faster. And, global diversification also reduces risk as American equity markets and international markets generally do not move together. Price movements between international and US asset classes are often dissimilar, so investing in both can increase your portfolio's diversification.

Dissimilar price movements are the name of the game, remember? Most of the stocks in a single country tend to be highly

FIGURE 10

Model Portfolio
Quarterly: 1973–2012

	Barclays US Govt./ Credit Bond Index	S&P 500 Index	BofA Merrill Lynch One-Year US Treasury Note Index	US Small Cap Index	US Large Cap Index	Targeted Value Index	Intl. Large Index	Intl. Small Index	Intl. Large Value Index	Intl. Small Value Index	Emerging Markets Blended Index	Annualized Compound Return
GOOD — Typical Portfolio	40%	60%										9.40%
STEP 1		60%	40%									8.67%
STEP 2		30%	40%	30%								9.48%
STEP 3		15%	40%	15%	15%	15%						10.35%
BEST — STEP 4 Target Portfolio		7.5%	40%	7.5%	7.5%	7.5%	6%	6%	6%	6%	6%	11.16%

correlated with each other. With the introduction of international asset classes, you gain greater downside protection by spreading your bets across different markets that have low correlation with each other. Investing in many different countries outside the US allows you to reduce risk and enhance returns with an additional dimension of diversification.

This is illustrated by the chart on the following pages. In many ways, this is a similar look to the diversification in asset classes that we just revisited, except this shows the returns by country over a twenty-five-year span.

FIGURE 11

Equity Returns of Developed Markets[20] Annual Return (%)

1988	1989	1990	1991	1992	1993	1994	1995	1996	1997	1998	1999	2000	
Belg. 53.63	Austria 103.91	UK 10.29	H.K. 49.52	H.K. 32.29	H.K. 116.70	Norway 23.57	Switz. 44.12	Spain 40.05	Switz. 44.25	Belg. 67.75	Sing. 99.40	Switz. 5.85	HIGH
Den. 52.67	Ger. 46.26	H.K. 9.18	Austral. 33.64	Switz. 17.23	Sing. 67.97	Japan 21.44	US 37.14	Sweden 37.21	Italy 35.48	Italy 52.52	Sweden 79.74	Can. 5.34	
Sweden 48.33	Norway 45.53	Austria 6.33	US 30.07	US 6.39	Switz. 45.79	Sweden 18.34	Sweden 33.36	H.K. 33.08	Den. 34.52	Spain 48.90	Japan 61.53	Den. 3.44	
Norway 42.40	Den. 43.94	Norway 0.65	Sing. 24.96	Sing. 6.28	Norway 42.04	Neth. 11.70	Spain 29.83	Norway 28.63	US 33.38	France 41.54	H.K. 59.52	Norway -0.89	
France 37.87	Sing. 42.26	Den. -0.91	France 17.83	France 2.81	Sweden 36.99	Italy 11.56	Neth. 27.71	Can. 28.54	Spain 25.41	US 30.14	Can. 53.74	Italy -1.33	
Austral. 36.40	France 36.15	US -3.15	Neth. 17.80	Neth. 2.39	Ger. 35.64	Belg. 8.24	Belg. 25.88	Neth. 27.51	Ger. 24.57	Ger. 29.43	Norway 31.70	Neth. -4.09	
Japan 35.39	Neth. 35.79	Neth. -3.19	Den. 16.56	Belg. -1.47	Neth. 35.28	Sing. 6.68	H.K. 22.57	UK 27.42	Neth. 23.77	Switz. 23.53	France 29.27	France -4.31	
Sing. 33.32	Sweden 31.79	Switz. -6.23	UK 16.02	UK -3.65	Austral. 35.17	Austral. 5.40	UK 21.27	US 23.24	UK 22.62	Neth. 23.23	US 21.92	Austral. -9.95	
H.K. 28.12	US 30.01	Ger. -9.36	Switz. 15.77	Den. -10.27	Den. 32.81	Ger. 4.66	Den. 18.78	Den. 21.79	Belg. 13.55	UK 17.80	Ger. 20.04	UK -11.53	
Ger. 20.60	Switz. 26.21	Belg. -10.98	Spain 15.63	Austria -10.65	Spain 29.78	Den. 3.77	Can. 18.31	France 21.20	Sweden 12.92	Sweden 13.96	Austral. 17.62	Austria -11.96	
Can. 17.07	Can. 24.30	Sing. -11.66	Sweden 14.42	Austral. -10.82	Italy 28.53	Switz. 3.54	Ger. 16.41	Austral. 16.49	Can. 12.80	Den. 8.99	UK 12.45	US -12.84	
US 14.61	UK 21.87	Can. -13.00	Belg. 13.77	Can. -12.15	Austria 28.09	US 1.13	France 14.12	Ger. 13.58	France 11.94	Austral. 6.07	Den. 12.06	H.K. -14.74	
Neth. 14.19	Italy 19.42	France -13.83	Can. 11.08	Sweden -14.41	Japan 25.48	UK -1.63	Austral. 11.19	Italy 12.59	Norway 6.24	Japan 5.05	Neth. 6.88	Ger. -15.59	
Spain 13.53	Belg. 17.29	Spain -13.85	Japan 8.92	Japan -21.45	UK 24.44	Can. -3.04	Sing. 6.45	Belg. 12.03	Austria 1.57	Austria 0.35	Spain 4.83	Spain -15.86	
Italy 11.46	Spain 9.76	Austral. -17.54	Ger. 8.16	Spain -21.87	Belg. 23.51	Spain -4.80	Norway 6.02	Austria 4.51	Austral. -10.44	H.K. -2.90	Italy -0.62	Belg. -16.85	
Switz. 6.18	Austral. 9.30	Italy -19.19	Italy -1.82	Italy -22.22	France 20.90	France -5.18	Italy 1.05	Switz. 2.28	H.K. -23.67	Can. -6.14	Switz. -7.02	Sweden -21.29	
UK 5.95	H.K. 8.39	Sweden -20.99	Austria -12.23	Norway -22.29	Can. 17.58	Austria -6.28	Japan 0.69	Japan -6.86	Japan -23.67	Sing. -12.88	Austria -9.11	Sing. -27.72	
Austria 0.57	Japan 1.71	Japan -36.10	Norway -15.50	Den. -28.25	US 9.15	H.K. -28.90	Austria -4.72	Japan -15.50	Sing. -30.05	Norway -30.06	Belg. -14.26	Japan -28.16	LOW

Similar to our experience with the chart of diverse asset classes, if we follow one country, say Austria (coded in white), we can see that that country has provided the *highest* percentage of returns three times and the *lowest* percentage of returns four times during the past twenty-five years. **The US (coded in black), on the other hand, has returned the highest annual return only twice during**

2001	2002	2003	2004	2005	2006	2007	2008	2009	2010	2011	2012	2013	
Austral. 1.68	Austria 16.55	Sweden 64.53	Austria 71.52	Can. 28.31	Spain 49.36	H.K. 41.20	Japan -29.21	Norway 87.07	Sweden 33.75	US 1.36	Belg. 39.55	US 31.80	HIGH
Austria -5.65	Austral. -1.34	Ger. 63.80	Belg. 43.53	Japan 25.52	Sing. 46.71	Ger. 35.21	Switz. -30.49	Austral. 76.43	Den. 30.73	UK -2.56	Den. 31.27	Ger. 31.40	
Belg. -10.89	Norway -7.26	Spain 58.46	Norway 38.39	Austria 24.64	Norway 45.12	Norway 31.43	US -37.57	Sing. 73.96	H.K. 23.23	Switz. -6.77	Sing. 30.96	Spain 31.30	
Spain -11.36	Italy -7.33	Austria 56.96	Sweden 36.28	Den. 24.50	Sweden 43.39	Can. 29.57	Spain -40.60	Sweden 64.16	Sing. 22.14	Norway -10.01	Ger. 30.90	Neth 31.30	
Norway -12.22	Japan -10.28	Can. 54.60	Italy 32.49	Norway 24.26	Den. 38.77	Sing. 28.35	France -43.27	H.K. 60.15	Can. 20.45	Belg. -10.62	H.K. 28.27	Den. 31.27	
US -12.39	Switz. -10.31	Austral. 49.46	Den. 30.82	Switz. 16.33	Belg. 36.66	Austral. 28.34	Can. -45.51	Belg. 57.49	Japan 15.44	Austral. -10.95	Austria 25.90	Belg. 27.60	
UK -14.05	Sing. -11.05	Den. 49.25	Austral. 30.34	Austral. 16.02	Austria 36.54	Den. 25.59	Ger. -45.87	Can. 56.18	US 14.77	Neth. -12.12	Austral. 22.07	Japan 27.20	
Den. -14.81	Can. -13.19	Norway 48.11	Spain 28.93	Sing. 14.37	Ger. 35.99	Spain 23.95	Sing. -47.35	Spain 43.48	Austral. 14.52	Spain -12.28	Sweden 21.97	Switz. 26.60	
H.K. -18.61	Belg. -14.97	France 40.22	H.K. 24.98	Neth. 13.85	France 34.48	Neth. 20.59	US -47.56	UK 46.30	Switz. 11.79	Can. -12.71	France 21.29	Sweden 24.50	
Can. -20.44	UK -15.23	H.K. 38.10	Sing. 22.27	Sweden 10.31	Italy 32.49	France 13.24	Neth. -48.22	Austria 43.20	Norway 10.95	Japan -14.33	Neth. 20.59	France 21.29	
Switz. -21.38	Spain -15.29	Italy 37.83	Can. 22.20	Ger. 9.92	Neth. 31.38	UK 8.36	UK -48.34	Neth. 42.26	Austria 9.88	Sweden -15.98	Switz. 20.35	UK 20.70	
Neth. -22.10	Den. -16.03	Sing. 37.60	UK 19.57	France 9.88	Austral. 30.86	Italy 6.06	Sweden -49.86	Den. 36.57	UK 8.76	Den. -16.02	Norway 18.65	Austria 13.40	
France -22.36	H.K. -17.79	Japan 35.91	France 18.48	Belg. 9.05	UK 30.61	US 5.44	Italy -49.98	France 31.83	Ger. 8.44	H.K. -16.02	US 15.33	Italy 12.48	
Ger. -22.39	Neth. -20.83	Belg. 35.33	Ger. 16.17	H.K. 8.40	H.K. 30.35	Switz. 5.29	Austral. -50.67	Italy 26.57	Neth. 1.74	France -16.87	UK 15.25	H.K. 11.10	
Sing. -23.42	France -21.18	Switz. 34.08	Japan 15.86	UK 7.35	Switz. 27.40	Austria 2.17	H.K. -51.21	US 26.25	Belg. -0.42	Sing. -17.92	Italy 12.48	Norway 9.40	
Italy -26.59	US -23.09	UK 32.06	Switz. 14.96	US 5.14	Can. 17.80	Sweden 0.62	Norway -64.24	Switz. 25.31	France -4.11	Ger. -18.08	Can. 9.09	Can. 5.60	
Sweden -27.18	Sweden -30.49	US 28.41	Neth. 12.24	Spain 4.41	US 14.67	Belg. -2.73	Belg. -66.48	Ger. 25.15	Italy -15.01	Italy -23.18	Japan 8.18	Austral. 4.20	LOW
Japan -29.40	Ger. -33.18	Neth. 28.09	US 10.14	Italy 1.90	Japan 6.24	Japan -4.23	Austria -68.41	Japan 6.25	Spain -21.95	Austria -36.43	Spain 3.00	Sing. 1.70	

this twenty-five-year span. If we insist on only investing in the US, we are simply going to miss out on so much growth. Many investors call the 2000s the "lost decade" as measured, for example, by the S&P 500 which returned nearly a zero percent growth from the years 2000–2010. Imagine the impact a zero percent return over ten years would have on your retirement. But, the fact is that during that time period, many investors experienced double-digit returns. The reason those investors did so well is because the rest of the world grew; if you held a globally diversified portfolio, it was far from a lost decade.

In the global context, I want to tell you a story about a client of mine that brings together a number of the things we have been talking about so far in this book. This is one of those everyday examples, far from unique, that illustrates the way many investors' minds work, maybe even yours?

In 2012, there was a time when the international markets were reeling. I got a lot of calls from my clients asking, "Why would I keep my money invested in Greece or Brazil when I'm hearing all this bad news about what is going on in their economies?" I went through my usual spiel (you know it by now!) that we have to be agnostic to what the markets are doing at the moment, ignore all of the noise generated by the media, and stick to our long-term goals. I wasn't trying to make light of why these news items were making certain clients nervous. But, I did want to remind them of all the conversations we had had up to this point, and how the next six or twelve months in one of the asset classes in which they were invested was going to be meaningless when viewed from the long-term of twenty or thirty years down the road.

Yet, I still had a client who didn't want to hear "this has happened many times in the past." Instead, he did what it is his right to do. He decided to take all of his money out of the international markets and convert those holdings to cash. In the end, I wouldn't stand in a client's way to do something like this. I give my best advice, but the client makes the decision at the end of the day.

Do I need to tell you what happened? This client happened to liquidate all of the international portions of his portfolio right at their lowest point. He took an unrealized loss—one that hasn't happened yet in reality, a loss on paper—*and turned it into a realized loss.* And, it was a significant loss.

Wouldn't you know it? By the end of the year, the international markets actually outperformed the US markets. And, here was a client who was making a significant difference in his life that he may never make up for. Taking money out on the downside, taking a realized loss, and losing all of that upside could severely impact any of our futures.

Diversification: The Bottom Line

It has been proven that over 92 percent of the time, the success of an investor's portfolio is directly tied into how well they have diversified, meaning how well an investor has allocated his or her portfolio among asset classes.[21] It's the old story of not putting all your eggs in one basket, so that you are effectively praying (anxiety) for that basket to come through for you. Through diversification, you don't have to be so attached to the fate of that one basket. You don't have to torture yourself with questions like: "Is the market too high right now to get back in? Is it the right time to invest?" In fact, diversification remains as close as there is to a free lunch!

By properly and effectively diversifying your portfolio, you create a very consistent investment experience, and there are very few cons to diversifying correctly. A well-diversified portfolio creates a dependable stream of income that will outpace inflation and keep up in any type of market condition. This, in turn, provides control over your finances in a way that you have never had before. Never again will you need to resort to anxiety where the market is concerned!

POINTS TO REMEMBER:

► Every year that your money is doing nothing for you it might as well be evaporating.

► Broad diversification means spreading the risk and reward within and among asset classes, capturing the full ride of all the sectors but with somewhat muted volatility at any given moment.

► Overseas investments can help you grow your wealth faster and reduce risk as American equity markets and international markets generally do not move together.

Chapter Four:
Goal-Setting

We all want control over our financial future, right? Whether that means taking care of our heirs, or giving charitably, or simply living as long as we can without having our money run out. How do we grow old with dignity and maintain our financial independence? That is our real goal. *Our real goal is not "how do I make as much money as I can in as short a period of time as possible?"* We know this, and yet sometimes the emotion of *envy* takes over, and it is this green monster that must be managed so that we can continue achieving the goals we have actually set.

If you're like me, you've heard a lot of people talk about their successes in the stock market. Maybe you've heard them at a backyard barbecue gloating, "I bought XYZ stock at however many dollars a share and now it's four times that. . . ." Why don't we ever hear people talk about their failures? You never hear people say things like, "I bought Google when it was $85 a share, but I sold it when it hit $120 . . . so, considering it's now over $800 and split last year, I probably lost about $200,000." Interesting, huh? Sometimes you will hear an individual talk about their losses. If you've ever heard William Shatner tell the story on Howard Stern about how he sold his Priceline.com shares for pennies on the dollar and lost millions, you have about as refreshing a perspective as you can find about a tragedy like that. The fact remains, most people don't talk about their miscues and many people try to package their successes in a way that is designed to make you feel jealous. And, it works.

The Smartest Man or Woman in the Room

One form of this envy that I see all the time is what also goes by the name of pride. *Remember, though, it doesn't really matter how smart you are. You can't be smarter than the market. Some of the smartest people in the world have tried and failed.* This is hard to accept for a number of my clients who are used to being the smartest person in the room. These individuals are business owners, doctors, accountants, and lawyers who own thriving practices. They are used to being the boss and doing things their way, and why not? Their drive and intelligence have created professional success and established a nice lifestyle for their families.

One of my clients, a very smart man, fit this profile to a T. Before we were introduced, he would make it his habit to extensively read the financial journals and would then buy up shares in the companies he'd read about. He constantly traded the market, so much so that when his portfolio went down he would trade even more using *leverage*. Leverage means establishing a special account with your brokerage firm so that you can actually borrow money from them to use for placing additional trades. For example, this individual had a $500,000 trading account, which meant he could borrow another $250,000. He would then invest that borrowed principal in an attempt to catch up.

By doing this, he was borrowing against his own assets, however, and this made it even worse than gambling! When you go to Las Vegas and lose your money, it's your money. Maybe you go to the ATM and take out more (which you know you shouldn't do), but it is still your money. When you trade using leverage and the markets go down, now you have not only lost your principal of $500,000, but you also owe the $250,000 back to the brokerage firm plus interest. *Leverage works great in up markets, but it will wipe you out in down markets.* Weaning this new client off of leverage was a task that my firm eventually accomplished, not by explaining the dangers of investing in this manner (those dangers were apparent enough to him), but by returning him to a focus on his **goals**. He wanted to provide a top-flight college education for his children, he wanted a vacation home at the beach where he and his wife could eventually retire, and he wanted to leave a charitable legacy for children afflicted with a rare disease, a cause close to his heart.

Getting clear on your goals is always the best way to begin achieving them. I didn't make that up! When it comes to investing, applying this particular wisdom sometimes appears as a kind of shock. You mean I shouldn't take out a home equity line of credit to place in highly speculative investments in the hope of recovering from recent losses? Right, you should not.

I had one couple come to me after a few years of our working together during which our returns had been steady: diversified across all asset classes to protect them from volatility while still maintaining a solid rate of growth—you know the drill by now. They wanted to ask me a bunch of questions about nontraded real estate investment trusts (REITs). They had been introduced to a gentleman who sold these REITs at a cocktail party (oh, those cocktail parties!) and they were about to pull the trigger and transfer all of their money to these nontraded REITs.

Such a move would have left them completely exposed to volatility. They were completely going after the big returns without any care to the level of risk they were taking. That's when I had to have what we call the "come to Jesus" meeting. We had to have a very difficult conversation in which I let them know that if they made this decision their lives could be affected forever. Of course, they had the final say in their portfolio; it's their money. Both of these individuals were attorneys so I explained it to them like someone hiring a lawyer. You might give input, but you don't tell the lawyer how to win your case. It's the same reason you go to an advisor: to delegate your financial planning and management to a qualified professional whom you trust. I reassured them that we were focusing on their real goals, needs, and priorities first—not on what kinds of products or services I have to sell.

I could tell they were getting aggravated with our stern tone. I'm fifty-years-old and they were both in their late sixties. But, you know what? They didn't transfer their money. Three weeks later, the SEC closed down the nontraded REITs for their high upfront fees, lack of transparency about how the companies value their real estate holdings, inherent conflicts of interest, and insufficient income to support its dividends. My attorney couple would have lost their entire investment, every penny.

Focus on Your Goals

The nontraded REIT debacle is really no different than a Ponzi scheme or the high-profile case of Bernie Madoff a few years ago. In all of these cases, investors are focusing on the wrong thing. **You don't focus on the return. You focus on the recipe that created that return.** How did they get that return? Then you focus on a different but related question: What are my goals? Your goals are probably not to "make as much money as you can in as short a period of time . . ." unless you want to finish that sentence with ". . . and leave yourself open to the possibility of losing more than you've earned and possibly losing it all."

In truth, your goals are probably something more concrete. Maybe you want a vacation home in the mountains, or you have achieved tremendous success in your career and want to leave behind an enduring legacy that will enable your favorite charity to continue its work. Maybe you want to give your children or grandchildren a great start in life, whether with a home or a business. We all want control over our financial future, whether that means taking care of our heirs, or giving charitably, or simply living as long as we can without having our money run out.

Consider the following list of five goals and see where you fit most closely. Bear in mind that these goals may overlap, but you can still get a sense of where your financial intentions really lie. Incidentally, this exercise is a good trial run for the Financial Life Map I will introduce in the next and final chapter.

GOAL NO. 1: Preserving wealth. Preserving wealth is pretty much what we have been talking about throughout this entire book. Slow and steady wins the race. Although many financial advisors think their main job is to create wealth, the great majority of affluent clients are much more concerned about losing their wealth. This was true even before the huge market disruption a few years ago, and it's become an even bigger issue since then. Clearly, having wealth doesn't erase or minimize the fear of losing what you have worked hard to build up over the years. Structured investing will take a risk, but only if it's a risk worth taking. It doesn't advocate taking no risks along the lines of my father-in-law, who was described in the previous chapter. If you recall, he lost out big to inflation because he never allowed himself to occasionally lose a little in the market and then follow with much larger gains. Nonetheless, I do regard one of my most important tasks to be assisting clients in preserving their wealth.

GOAL NO. 2: Mitigating taxes. Taxes may be, as Oliver Wendell Holmes once said, "the price we pay for a civilized society."[22] But that doesn't mean investors look forward to paying for those privileges. In fact, mitigating income taxes is a concern of more than 90 percent of those clients that we work with, along with mitigating estate and capital gains taxes. Remember, it's not how much money you make. It's how much money you keep. It's always been that way!

As a response to this, my firm has developed innovative ways of bringing other experts into the mix. (This is part of "comprehensive wealth management," which we will discuss in the next chapter.) We're not CPAs, but we're smart enough to bring a CPA into the mix. Mitigating taxes might take the form of investing in special tax advantage funds, or simply staying up to date with changes to the tax laws. For example, a couple of years ago, you could leave **$1.2 million to each heir tax-free.** Then that law was changed so that you can now leave each individual $5 million. A big difference! Your estate plan needs to be updated with these changes in mind, and your advisor should be able to take the lead on this.

GOAL NO. 3: Taking care of heirs. As I mentioned, a number of these goals overlap, and, in the previous item, we saw the importance of staying on top of shifting tax laws for the benefit of one's descendants. Approximately 80 percent of our clients said that a major concern was ensuring that their heirs, parents, children, and grandchildren are taken care of with minimal difficulty and cost and in accordance with their wishes. Yet, the majority of these clients had estate plans that were more than three-years-old when they came to us. Why?

Many people ignore this crucial concern for too long because addressing it requires them to ask potentially uncomfortable questions about mortality and family issues. However, failing to ensure that wealth goes exactly where our clients want it to go can have big ramifications when it comes to achieving their goals of succession and sustainability.

GOAL NO. 4: Protecting one's assets. Many of our investors want to protect their assets from being unjustly taken by potential creditors, litigants, ex-spouses, and children's spouses. In addition, nearly half of all the clients we surveyed were worried about being sued. The wealthier you are, the more exposed you are to all of these different things that may take your money away one day. This means that wealth-management planning must also address controlling risks though business processes, employment agreements, and buy-sells, as well as restructuring various assets and considering legal forms of ownership—trusts, limited liability entities, and so on—that put wealth beyond the reach of creditors and other parties.

Just the other day, we met with a client who is an attorney and owns multiple properties in his own name. We had to explain to him just how wrong this was. If someone slips and falls in front of one of his buildings, they could take everything from him, as opposed to if he owned the properties through an LLC, which would protect his assets. This is where working with an advisor who does comprehensive wealth management comes into play; having a team of people who can help our clients understand just how underinsured they are or how they are insured in the wrong ways.

GOAL NO. 5: Charitable gifting. Increasingly, our clients are looking beyond their own families to the world at large. For approximately 30 percent of them, making meaningful gifts to charity is a key issue. Charitable gifting comes with its own unique challenges, of course—from selecting causes and specific organizations that will have the biggest impact to balancing the desire to leave a legacy with the need to provide for the near future. Charitable gifts can be a valuable component of an investor's overall tax and estate plan, while still living up to the words of an anonymous writer: "We make a living by what we get, but we make a life by what we give."[23]

Four ways for a smart investor to make charitable contributions to their favorite causes are: start a family foundation, which is a great way to get children and grandchildren involved with the family's philanthropic efforts; donate highly appreciated stocks so that you can derive an income for life from these assets without having to pay capital gains on the sale of the stock; using a Donor Advised Fund (DAF) account, which is similar to an investment account except that it is earmarked exclusively for charitable giving; and donating from an Individual Retirement Account (IRA).

Did you see yourself on the list? Discerning your true goals will help you and your advisor immeasurably in the task of deciding which investments are right for you and your overall level of risk tolerance. Getting clear on your goals is also the best antidote to envy that I know of, focusing on yourself and your family rather that yourself in comparison with others.

POINTS TO REMEMBER:

► It doesn't matter how smart you are—you can't be smarter than the market.

► Don't focus on the return, focus on the recipe that created that return.

► Structured investing will take a risk, but only if it's a risk worth taking.

Chapter Five:

Choosing the Right Advisor for You

In each of the four previous chapters, we saw how a negative emotion attached to investing can be replaced by a positive one:

- Our *impatience* for overly rapid growth which leaves us exposed can be effectively countered by **patience**.

- Our *regret* over trying to time the market (buying low and selling high) can be eliminated by following a **discipline**.

- Our *anxiety* over what tomorrow might bring to our portfolio can be addressed by proper **diversification**.

- Our *envy* over other people's supposed gains dissipates when we focus on our own personal **goals**.

In this chapter, I want to talk about two final emotions that await you at the end of this journey: **courage** and **peace**. The courage I speak of is the courage to take control of your own finances—and to realize it is never too late to do so. The peace is that feeling that ensues when you are enriched, secure, and whole: all words that apply just as well to an emotional state of mind as to a positive financial reality!

Courage: It's Never Too Late

Let's begin with courage. You may belong to the vast majority of the population who feels unprepared to retire. You may have a safety net but live a lifestyle which is too luxurious for your current needs. You may be a business owner who wakes up one day and says, "I want to sell my business tomorrow." You may not even be sure of what securities you are currently invested in, or how they compare to other possibilities. Now, can you wake up tomorrow and change all of that? There is a lot of planning that needs to go into portfolio transformation, just as there is a lot of planning that goes into paying off debt, business succession, establishing proper long-term care insurance, and saving through work retirement plans. But, no matter how far behind the eight ball you may feel, you can always get back on track. The important thing to know is that there is a right way to "catch up" and a wrong way.

The key to successful investing, as we have seen throughout this book, is to find the proper balance between risk and return, neither investing too conservatively nor too aggressively. Most investors have no idea how to do that and instead take way too much risk trying to make up for those lost years. This inevitably sets the well-intentioned investor back even further, especially if they don't understand the risks they are taking. There are other options besides trying to catch up by taking more risks. Those options include: making lifestyle changes, working more years, or working part-time for a period of time instead of entering full retirement. Echoing the theme of this book, if you can control your behavior, you can achieve your financial goals. With courage, and the proper advisor, you can put together a plan that will enable you to move securely in the direction you intend.

Finding a Broker: What to Look for

The pitfalls for investors who do not adequately prepare for retirement can be scary; basically, you will outlive your money. With effective, ongoing communications between client and advisor, however, a grounded plan can be put in place that will provide the answer to successful investing and a carefree retirement. But, where do you begin to find the right advisor for you? You might begin your search online or through someone in your professional or personal network that you trust. Once you uncover a referral, I would use every means possible to investigate this person. Google his or her name, check their Facebook page, their LinkedIn recommendations, and their Twitter account. In these days of social media and web-archived data, you can get a tremendous amount of information about a person, not only what they say about themselves, but also what other people say about them. Do as much research as you can, remembering that you must get to know your advisor almost as intimately as the person you want to marry and spend the rest of your life with! After all, this will be one of the most intimate relationships you will ever have.

Once you have a solid lead for a broker you are interested in working with, there are five quick and easy questions to answer before proceeding forward with this individual.

1. **Can they offer at least five references?** I am always shocked at how many people don't follow-through on calling references that are offered. Now, obviously this advisor is going to give you great clients to call, but you can do your due diligence. Ask difficult but friendly questions such as: "If you were invested with this advisor in 2008, did she or he run and hide when the markets got bad?" "Are they transparent, or do they conceal key pieces of information?" There

is a limit to the amount of information you, as an investor, need. You don't have to be overeducated about wealth management, but you don't want information kept from you, either. Is their practice high or low touch? And, lastly, and this may be the hardest to quantify, does the referral you are speaking with feel that the advisor cares?

2. **Has the advisor been in business for at least ten years?** Has he or she been through both bear markets and bull markets, weathering enough recessions to be a competent guide for the long term? Many investors don't give enough credit to experience and are too attracted to educational credentials instead. A fancy diploma does only so much to prepare you for the battle. Instead, you want the equivalent of a surgeon who has done the same surgery a thousand times; she or he is prepared for everything that can happen on that table.

3. **Is the advisor "fee only"?** That is, do they charge by the hour or receive an annual fee, rather than being paid by commission? Commissions are the lifeblood of Wall Street and, as we have seen, they are the root of conflict of interest between advisor and client. How can an advisor have the client's best interests at heart when they are compensated by the products they sell as opposed to how well those investments succeed? (As a corollary to this, there should never be a "break-up fee" or a certain time period before you are able to leave an advisor.)

4. **Does the advisor offer comprehensive wealth management?** Many financial firms say they offer wealth management, but providing investment management with maybe a little college education and estate planning is insufficient. True

comprehensive wealth management should address your entire range of financial issues. I will discuss this in more detail later in the chapter.

5. **Does the advisor have a discipline that unfolds in a specific process which they can show you in writing?** You know me well enough by now to know how important I think it is to have such a discipline, and it will become very clear to you whether this advisor has such a process in place or not. In fact, I think it's so important I'm going to devote the entire next section to it!

A Process in Place

By this point in your reading, you probably have a better sense of what you are looking for in an advisor: someone who believes in transparency; a decisive, focused, receptive, optimistic individual who offers a full-range of financial services; someone who has your best interests at heart and is not motivated by a conflict in interest. The single most important thing your advisor should have is a clear direction represented by a process they can show you, a process that they've engaged in for years. In addition, your advisor needs to be able to articulate this process, a conversation which should unfold over a series of meetings, and they need to be able to adapt this process to uncover your true financial needs and goals to craft a long-term plan. This is because everyone is different.

The advisor with whom you decide to work should take your unique needs and preferences into account. At CJM Wealth, our first meeting is always a **discovery meeting**. What is the prospective client's current situation? What obstacles do they face in achieving their goals? I take care not to overwhelm someone at first, but I do want them to realize that we are looking at the entire picture. I have found it is easier to visualize this rather than to talk about it in the abstract, so during the discovery meeting I present the prospective client with the following Financial Life Map. I ask them to rank the categories on the top line from highest to lowest importance (i.e., Is creating financial comfort more or less important than building a legacy?, etc.) Then, we do the same within each category, ranking each item from highest to lowest importance.

FIGURE 12

Financial Life Map

Helping and protecting family	Enjoying and protecting lifestyle	Planning ahead	Creating financial comfort	Building a legacy
Helping children	Income needs	Clarifying vision	Managing resources	Will and power of attorney
Assisting parents	Leisure planning	Health challenges	Generating income	Estate transfer
Funding education	Personal health	Managing change	Minimizing taxes	Charitable giving
Retirement transition planning	Protecting assets and business	Life transition planning	Working with an advisory team	Living legacy

Source: Loring Ward

This "360 degree" discovery process ensures that our wealth management program matches the client's goals, and not only so that we can make the best initial recommendations, but also so that we can stay on track throughout our hopefully long and fruitful affiliation. The client has to come first—these aren't empty words. An advisor simply has to discover what is important to the client and where their priorities lie.

The second meeting is called the **investment plan meeting**. During this meeting, we present a complete diagnostic of the client's current financial situation and a plan for achieving their investment-related goals. Sometimes I'm asked the question, "You designed this plan just for me, but how do I know that it isn't cookie cutter?" Well, honestly, some of it is cookie cutter, if by that you mean that we use the concentrated research of our entire team to make the same recommendations for investment strategy to many of our clients. On the other hand, it will be completely unique, because it is tailored to your unique responses to the Financial Life Map. In my experience it has never happened that any individual ranks the twenty categories on this chart in the exact same order as someone else!

The third meeting with a prospective client is called the **mutual commitment meeting**. This is when we officially decide to work together: we've already done all of the legwork, gathering statements and filling out paperwork. We've reviewed what we're going to do, the way we're going to do it, when we're going to do it, and what the costs are. The client wants me as an advisor, and I have made sure they have all their questions answered to take this step. Prospective clients can ask me anything (and have!). They might ask, "Well, are you going to be handling my portfolio, or is someone else going to be handling it?" To which I respond, "When you say 'handling,' we have a team in place: one part is going to handle the administrative portion, one part is going to handle the operational portion, and I am going to handle the relationship portion. It's broken up by responsibility, but it's one seamless team." The clients might then ask, "Well, am I going to meet all of those people?" The answer to that question is yes! By this point in the process most clients already have. Or, a prospect might ask me, "How many clients do you work with at one time? How do I know you aren't going to take on more clients than you can handle?" Again, I answer this question by referring to the team we have in place. What the client really wants to know is: "Do you have a system in place whereby I will receive the customer service I deserve?" The answer is: "Try us and see. When you do, you will see you always get a call back within twenty-four hours and in most cases much sooner if there is a matter that is to any degree time-sensitive."

This notion of the team is carried through in the next meetings that occur, the **regular process meetings**. These are typically held quarterly, where we report on the progress a client is making and hear about important changes in your life that might call for an adjustment to your investment plan. It is also at these meetings where we reveal the blueprint for addressing a client's advanced planning needs that has been developed in coordination with a network of experts—what is known as comprehensive wealth management. To better understand what comprehensive wealth management is all about, I think it is useful to view the components to wealth management (WM) in terms of the following formula:

$$WM = IC + AP + RM$$

IC here represents investment consulting, the piece that you may be the most familiar with—what we have spent the majority of this book discussing. To fulfill this role, your advisor helps you build a diversified, efficient portfolio of securities that undergo periodic rebalancing, a portfolio designed for maximal gain with minimal volatility, fees, and taxes. There are other elements of successful wealth management to consider as well, such as: advanced planning (AP), which includes wealth enhancement, wealth transfer, wealth protection, and charitable giving; and relationship management (RM) which connects the investor with other financial professionals, such as attorneys and accountants who possess specialized expertise. Because no one person can be an expert in every subject, the best wealth managers work with networks of experts: financial professionals with deep experience and knowledge in specific areas.

Peace: The Leap of Faith

Every investor-advisor relationship requires a leap of faith. No investor wants to hand their portfolio off to someone whom they don't trust or with whom they don't connect. Once you do find an advisor whom you can rely on implicitly, someone who can become your own personal CFO, then you want to be able to take full advantage of this relationship. **This is where the emotion of peace comes in, as in peace of mind.**

Peace surrounding your financial picture can be yours when you have the courage to make the right decisions for yourself and for your family. As an informed investor, you always want to navigate the extremes between simply handing off your wealth management entirely and feeling the need to be hypervigilant which often leads to rushed and ill-informed decisions.

Between these two hazards lies the "smooth sailing" that comes from working with the right advisor, someone who never takes lightly the responsibility of having you as a client. When you find that advisor it should promote these feelings of courage and peace as you see the joy they take in doing business. A new client recently sent me this email after leaving my office, and I think it well describes the impact I am trying to make:

> *"Charlie, thanks once again for the productive and instructive meeting today, I can't tell you how much of a sense of relief I have after hearing your thoughts about growing our nest egg over the next years. I am thankful for our relationship and your wise stewardship."*

Your advisor should not only constantly look for ways to add value, he or she should also be someone who will never give up, and who will always put much more into a client relationship than she or he will ever get back. Everyone has someone they care so deeply about that they would do anything for them, and when we are talking about your long-term financial security, the stakes simply couldn't be higher. Find someone passionate about making a difference in your life so you can make a difference in the lives of others.

POINTS TO REMEMBER:

► It is never too late to take control of your own finances.

► The key to successful investing is to find the proper balance between risk and return, and not taking too much risk trying to make up for lost years.

► The single most important thing a prospective advisor should be able to show you is a clear direction represented by a process they have engaged in for years.

Endnotes

[1] Rieker, Matthias. "UBS, Popular Sued Over Losses in Puerto Rico Bond Funds." *The Wall Street Journal*, May 7, 2014. Accessed June 12, 2014. http://online.wsj.com/news/articles/SB10001424052702303701304579548293034531248. *See also:* Zamansky, Jake. "Created By UBS, Muni Bond 'Perfect Storm' Now Over Island Of Puerto Rico." *Forbes*, October 7, 2013. Accessed June 12, 2014. http://www.forbes.com/sites/jakezamansky/2013/10/07/created-by-ubs-muni-bond-perfect-storm-now-over-island-of-puerto-rico/

[2] Lucchetti, Aaron and Jean Eaglesham. "Morgan Stanley Gets Facebook Fine." *The Wall Street Journal,* December, 18, 2012. Accessed June 12, 2014. http://online.wsj.com/news/articles/SB10001424127887324407504578185580869680410.

[3] A fiduciary is a person, such as an investment manager or the executor of an estate, or an organization, such as a bank, entrusted with the property of another party and in whose best interests the fiduciary is expected to act when holding, investing, or otherwise using that party's property.

[4] Schwartz, Nelson D. "The Ugly Truth About IPOs." *Fortune*, November 23, 1998. Accessed June 12, 2014. http://money.cnn.com/magazines/fortune/fortune_archive/1998/11/23/251436/index.htm

[5] French, Kenneth R. "The Cost of Active Investing." April 9, 2008. Available at SSRN: http://ssrn.com/abstract=1105775 or http://dx.doi.org/10.2139/ssrn.1105775.

[6] Figure 1: Bowen, John J., Jr., Patricia J. Abram, and Jonathan Powell. *Breaking Through: Building a World Class Wealth Management Business.* CEG Worldwide, 2008.

[7] Lauricella, Tom. "The Stock Picker's Defeat." *The Wall Street Journal,* December 10, 2008. Accessed June 12, 2014. http://online.wsj.com/news/articles/SB122886123425292617

[8] Figure 2: Data Sources: S&P 500, MSCI EAFE Index, FTSE NAREIT Equity REITs, MSCI Pacific ex Japan Index, MSCI Emerging Markets Index, IA SBBI US Inflation Index: Morningstar Direct. Fama/French US Small Value Index (ex utilities), Small Growth Index (ex utilities), Large Value Index (ex utilities), Large Growth Index (ex utilities), Five-Year US Treasury Notes: Dimensional Returns version 2.3, March 2014. All investments involve risk, including the loss of principal and cannot be guaranteed against loss by a bank, custodian, or any other financial institution. Foreign securities involve additional risks, including foreign currency changes, political risks, foreign taxes, and different methods of accounting and financial reporting. Past performance is not indicative of future performance. Treasury notes are guaranteed as to repayment of principal and interest by the US government. This information does not constitute a solicitation for sale of any securities. S&P 500 Index is the Standard & Poor's 500 Index. The S&P 500 Index measures the performance of large-capitalization US stocks. The S&P 500 is an unmanaged market value-weighted index of 500 stocks that are traded on the NYSE, AMEX and NASDAQ. The weightings make each company's influence on the index performance directly proportional to that company's market value. The MSCI EAFE Index (Morgan Stanley Capital International Europe, Australasia, Far East Index) is comprised of over 1,000 companies representing the stock markets of Europe, Australia, New Zealand and the Far East, and is an unmanaged index. EAFE represents non-US large stocks. Consumer

Price Index (CPI) is a measure of inflation. REITs, represented by the NAREIT Equity REIT Index, is an unmanaged, market cap-weighted index comprised of 151 equity REITS. Emerging Markets index represents securities in countries with developing economies and provide potentially high returns. Many Latin American, Eastern European and Asian countries are considered emerging markets. Indexes are unmanaged baskets of securities without the fees and expenses associated with mutual funds and other investments. Investors cannot directly invest in an index. LWI Financial Inc. ("Loring Ward") is an investment adviser registered with the Securities and Exchange Commission. Securities transactions may be offered through Loring Ward Securities Inc., an affiliate, member FINRA/SIPC. IRN R 13-091 (Exp 3/15). Diversification does not guarantee a profit or protect against a loss.

[9] Richards, Carl. "Forget Market Timing, and Stick to a Balanced Fund." *New York Times*, January 27, 2014. Accessed June 12, 2014. http://www.nytimes.com/2014/01/28/your-money/forget-market-timing-and-stick-to-a-balanced-fund.html?_r=0.

[10] Parkman, Bob. "Consider These 'Words of Wisdom' About Investing." *Sir John Templeton*, September 20, 2006. Accessed June 12, 2014. http://www.sirjohntempleton.org/articles_details.asp?a=16.

[11] "Dow Jones Industrial Average All-Time Largest One Day Gains and Losses." *The Wall Street Journal*. Accessed June 12, 2014. http://online.wsj.com/mdc/public/page/2_3024-djia_alltime.html.

[12] Figure 5: Indices are not available for direct investment. Their performance does not reflect the expenses associated with the management of an actual portfolio. Past performance is not a guarantee of future results. In US dollars. Performance data for January 1970–August 2008 provided by CRSP; performance data for September 2008–December 2013 provided by Bloomberg. The S&P data are provided by Standard

& Poor's Index Services Group. US bonds and bills data © Stocks, Bonds, Bills, and Inflation Yearbook™, Ibbotson Associates, Chicago (annually updated work by Roger G. Ibbotson and Rex A. Sinquefield).

[13] French, Kenneth R. "The Cost of Active Investing." April 9, 2008. Available at SSRN: http://ssrn.com/abstract=1105775 or http://dx.doi.org/10.2139/ssrn.1105775.

[14] Barras, Laurent, O. Scaillet, and Russ Wermers. "False Discoveries in Mutual Fund Performance: Measuring Luck in Estimated Alphas." April 20, 2009. Robert H. Smith School Research Paper No. RHS 06-043. Available at SSRN: http://ssrn.com/abstract=869748.

[15] Figure 8: Barras, Laurent, O. Scaillet, and Russ Wermers. "False Discoveries in Mutual Fund Performance: Measuring Luck in Estimated Alphas." April 20, 2009. Robert H. Smith School Research Paper No. RHS 06-043. Available at SSRN: http://ssrn.com/abstract=869748.

[16] US Energy Information Administration. "Weekly US Regular All Formulations Retail Gasoline Prices (Dollars per Gallon)." Accessed June 12, 2014. http://www.eia.gov/dnav/pet/hist/LeafHandler.ashx?f=W&n=PET&s=EMM_EPMR_PTE_NUS_DPG

[17] Markowitz, Harry M. *Portfolio Selection: Efficient Diversification of Investments.* Malden, Massachusetts: Blackwell Publishers, 1991.

[18] The "Fama and French Three Factor Model" expands on the capital asset pricing model (CAPM) by adding size and value factors in addition to the market risk factor in CAPM. This model considers the fact that value and small cap stocks outperform markets on a regular basis. By including these two additional factors, the model adjusts for the outperformance tendency, which is thought to make it a better tool for evaluating manager performance.

[19] Siegel, Jeremy J. *Impact of an Aging Population on the Global Economy.* CFA Institute Conference Proceedings Quarterly, September 2007.

Accessed June 12, 2014. http://www.cfapubs.org/doi/pdf/10.2469/cp.v24.n3.4846.

[20] Figure 11: In US dollars. Source: MSCI developed markets country indices (net dividends) with at least twenty-five years of data. MSCI data copyright MSCI 2014, all rights reserved; see MSCI disclosure page for additional information. Indices are not available for direct investment. Index performance does not reflect expenses associated with the management of an actual portfolio. Past performance is not a guarantee of future results.

[21] Larrabee, David. "Setting the Record Straight on Asset Allocation." *Enterprising Investor.* CFA Institute. *February* 16, 2012. Accessed June 12, 2014. http://blogs.cfainstitute.org/investor/2012/02/16/setting-the-record-straight-on-asset-allocation/

[22] Compania General De Tabacos De Filipinas v. Collector of Internal Revenue, 275 U.S. 87, 100, dissenting opinion (21 November 1927).

[23] Quote often falsely attributed to Winston Churchill. https://www.winstonchurchill.org/learn/speeches/quotations/quotes-falsely-attributed

Acknowledgements

Getting Off the Street was not conceived as an investment how-to book. It was written out of the passion I have for helping people do more of what they love with those they love most. This is something that most investment firms lose sight of, however, as I approach my 52nd birthday it has never been clearer in my life.

I have been blessed to be surrounded by so many people who have supported me and believed in me both personally and professionally.

I begin with my clients, who are truly an extension of my own family. If not for their trust and confidence in allowing me to manage their family's financial future and security, my career (and hence, this book!) would not be possible.

I have been fortunate since starting CJM to have a tremendous team of people assist with our growth who share the same commitment for our clients. Especially Peter and Diane who have felt the growing pains but also celebrated our many distinctions.

My Mom and Dad, Marie and Pat, always held a silent faith in everything I did. When I was a child, they allowed me to stumble along the way which allowed me to become the man I am today.

My fourteen-year-old boys, Christopher and Steven, teach me every day through their autism and big smiles, that life is never predictable but always fun. My daughter, Elaina, is everything I could have hoped for and more in a young lady.

My final and biggest acknowledgment goes to my wife — and biggest cheerleader — Stella. I cannot picture a life without her. Many people have made this book possible, but she has made *everything* possible.

I believe with all my heart and soul that *Getting Off the Street* can empower people to take control of their finances like never before, leading to the most successful investment experience of their lives. Then, they also can spend the majority of their time doing the things they love with the people they love most.

About the Author

President and Founder, Charlie Massimo started his career in 1984 as a compliance officer at Shearson Lehman Brothers. He moved to New York Life Insurance Company as a senior representative and later joined Merrill Lynch as a financial consultant in the Private Client Group. In 1999, he moved to Smith Barney as vice president of investments.

While his career was advancing, Charlie became aware of the diverging intents between his employers and their clients: one seeking to sell product, the other desiring a sustainable portfolio. Determined to run a firm that put the interests of its clients above everything else, Charlie took a leap of faith and founded CJM Wealth Management in 2003. The firm now manages over $300 million in client assets and has been named the *Premier Wealth Management Company on Long Island* by NABCAP and been listed in the 2014 volume of *America's Select Financial Advisors*.

Married and the father of triplets, one daughter and two sons who are both on the autism spectrum, Charlie realizes that each of his clients has a vision for their life and the lives of their loved ones.

One of the hallmarks of Charlie's vision is his professional fulfillment born of knowing he has helped his clients achieve their financial goals, build the life they desire, and benefit from having a trusted advisor with whom they enjoy a warm, open relationship.